IMAGINE

DEMOCRACY

IMAGINE
DEMOCRACY

JUDY REBICK

Stoddart

Published in 2000 by Stoddart Publishing Co. Limited
34 Lesmill Road, Toronto, Canada M3B 2T6

Distributed by:
General Distribution Services Ltd.
325 Humber College Blvd., Toronto, Canada M9W 7C3
Tel. (416) 213-1919   Fax (416) 213-1917
Email cservice@genpub.com

04 03 02 01 00   1 2 3 4 5

Canadian Cataloguing in Publication Data

Rebick, Judy
Imagine democracy

Includes index.
ISBN 0-7737-3229-2

1. Canada — Politics and government — 1993–   .*
2. Democracy.   I. Title.

FC635.R42 2000   971.064'8   C00-930041-4
F1034.2.R42 2000

Jacket design: Angel Guerra
Text design: Kinetics Design & Illustration

THE CANADA COUNCIL | LE CONSEIL DES ARTS
FOR THE ARTS | DU CANADA
SINCE 1957 | DEPUIS 1957

We acknowledge for their financial support of our publishing
program the Canada Council, the Ontario Arts Council, and
the Government of Canada through the Book Publishing
Industry Development Program (BPIDP).

Printed and bound in Canada

TO DAN LECKIE

1949–1998

A true democrat

*The radical, committed to human liberation,
does not become the prisoner of a circle of certainty
within which reality is also imprisoned. On the
contrary, the more radical the person is, the more fully
he or she enters into reality so that, knowing it better,
he or she can better transform it.*

— PAULO FREIRE, *Pedagogy of the Oppressed*

Contents

ACKNOWLEDGEMENTS

THE IDEAS IN THIS BOOK COME, first and foremost, from my political experience, particularly my three extraordinarily intense years as president of Canada's largest women's group. My first thank-you goes to the women I worked with on the National Action Committee on the Status of Women over those years, especially Barbara Cameron, Sandra Delaronde, Shelagh Day, and Salome Loucas, who worked on our constitutional committee; Sunera Thobani, Carolann Wright, Fele Villasin, Winnie Ng, and Kiké Roach, who taught me a lot about power, racism, and equality; and Monique Simard, who provided such an important link with Quebec.

The ideas of many others fill these pages, but two people stand out. Hilary Wainwright and Leo Panitch have long insisted on the centrality of democratization to the socialist project. They both provided a theoretical framework for ideas that were emerging from my own political experience. I also thank all the other people you will meet in these pages who so generously shared their time, experience, and wisdom.

I am grateful to those who made the writing and production of the book possible. My agent, Linda McKnight, helped me organize my ideas into a saleable project and continues to guide me through the world of publishing. Robert Chodos, who was my first writing partner at the *McGill Daily* in 1966, read an early draft and provided much-needed suggestions. Barbara Cameron, a friend and comrade, took time to give me political feedback on the manuscript. Jack Stoddart and Don Bastian have kindly provided a mechanism for getting these ideas out to a broader audience. And my editor Janice Weaver calmly and expertly helped shape my words into what I hope is an eminently readable book.

And finally, my thanks to Terra, Lucas, Kael, and Gabe, who keep me young and try to keep me humble.

Needless to say, I alone am responsible for the contents of what you are about to read. Enjoy.

INTRODUCTION

FOR MY WHOLE LIFE, politics has been my passion. When I use the word "politics," I'm referring not to the sterile, partisan role-playing that you see in the House of Commons, but to the sometimes thrilling, sometimes painful process of struggling for social change. Indeed, the most joyful moments of my life have come in hard-fought political victories, in pushing an issue onto the public agenda, in planting the seeds for a demonstration and watching it grow, and in collaborating with men and women whose friendship has been forged in common struggle.

I have been part of causes that fundamentally changed the course of history, such as the anti–Vietnam War protests and the women's movement. I have led struggles that made life better for women in Canada, including the fight to decriminalize abortion and the one to strengthen the rape law. I have participated in battles that stayed the hand of government, such as the campaign against the Charlottetown Accord. I've worked in solidarity with some of the most oppressed people in Canada — aboriginal and disabled people — and gained inspiration from their spirit and their joy in life. And of course I've fought some losing battles, too, such as those over the Free Trade Agreement and employment equity, where people with no formal power still managed to make their voices heard and even mobilize public opinion.

Yet lately my passion for social change is in danger of growing cold. These days, the mobilization of even thousands of people, as happened during the Days of Action protests against the right-wing savagery of Mike Harris's Conservative government in Ontario, seems to have only a momentary impact. Teachers can organize and fight magnificently to protect public education, only to see it eroded anyway. Moderate groups like nurses' unions are forced into illegal action just to maintain a decent standard of living and a minimal level of service. And I never thought I would see the day when so many people in Canada's major cities were forced to live on the streets.

Political parties are starting to look more and more like each other. Instead of being given real policy options, we are asked to choose from among savage right-wing politics with no excuse, à la Mike Harris; savage right-wing politics with a smile and a look of concern, à la Jean Chrétien; and pallid centre-right politics with a shrug, à la Bob Rae. Almost every person in public life, whatever his or her political inclination, tells us that there are no alternatives. We have to accept cutbacks to social programs, massive inequities between rich and poor, unbridled greed in the private sector, we are told, because there is nothing else.

In my youth, there were many alternatives. We could look to the south and gain inspiration from the American civil-rights movement, or look farther south, to the revolutionary people's movements of Cuba and Chile. We could look to the east and the massive Chinese and Russian revolutions, which took people from the dire poverty of feudalism into the modern world. Despite the brutality and authoritarianism with which these revolutions were implemented, the ideas of economic equality that underlay them were inspirational. We could look to Europe and the brilliant student uprising in France, which won the support of workers for a more just society. Ideas poured out of these manifold struggles like a water-fall. It was dizzying and exciting to figure out where you stood.

Thirty years later, the flow of progressive ideas seems to have slowed to a trickle. Fiscal responsibility and lower taxes have replaced peace and love as the signature of my generation. The culture of our movements for social justice has been co-opted by mutual funds and banks. What a feeling of despair came over me when I saw the Bank of Montreal use one of my generation's classic anthems, Bob Dylan's "The Times They Are A-Changin'," to sell computer banking. Our rhetoric has even been captured by centre-left governments to justify war, as happened with the NATO bombings of Kosovo, when old-fashioned Western power politics was cloaked in the language of humanitarian intervention.

The problem is not only that the capitalist elite has recovered from its momentary lapse of total control, but also that it has done so by seriously restricting the democratic space. Globalization, as it has come to be called (or more accurately, neo-liberalism), is well on the way to creating a world in its own image. Countries find that their freedom to develop their own economic strategies is restricted by a three-part vise that includes free-trade agreements, uncontrolled investment capital, and institutions like the ones that came out of the 1944 Bretton Woods conference, the International Monetary Fund (IMF) and the World Bank. A country that doesn't follow the neo-liberal orthodoxy — privatize, deregulate, eliminate the deficit, cut taxes, and reduce social services — pays a heavy, if not catastrophic, price. For developed countries, this price includes serious loss of investment income, higher interest on loans, trade embargoes, and other economic sanctions; for developing countries, it's ineligibility for IMF and World Bank financing. If countries do follow the orthodoxy, the consequent reduction of the public sector puts even more power in the hands of the corporate elite. Organizations from theatre groups to schools have to rely on private capital, which grows exponentially while public wealth shrinks by the day.

I call this trend postmodern feudalism. In feudal times, the serfs had to rely on the beneficence of the lord. Today, we have to rely on the beneficence of corporations. In a few short years, we moved from allowing Pepsi-Cola machines in our school cafeterias to embracing television news in the classroom (with content that won't offend advertisers, of course) — all so our cash-strapped schools can get equipment. How long before we accept curricula produced by corporations, as they already are in some American schools? After a speech I gave to a group of teachers in Toronto, one principal asked me, "What choice do we have but to work with corporations? Where else are we to get the funding that we need?" I was amazed that even these educators, who were strong supporters of public education, were already spending more of their energy searching for private funding than fighting to restore a satisfactory level of public funding. Over time, the fiscal necessity of going begging to private corporations for public needs becomes normalized. As governments provide fewer and deteriorating services, more and more citizens resent having to pay for them and start supporting demands for lower taxes.

Nowhere is the impact of this postmodern feudalism more obvious than in the media. Corporate concentration of the media, always a problem, has grown to such major proportions that it raises serious questions about the meaning of freedom of the press. How could there be political diversity in print media when in most cities we can choose only between Conrad Black's newspaper and Lord Thomson's? The obsession with maximizing profit has also seized our electronic media. If it were not for the Canadian Radio-television and Telecommunications Commission (CRTC), which no doubt many right-wingers would love to see eliminated, our private television stations would probably broadcast American television programs exclusively. News and public-affairs programming is being starved of needed resources on every network, including the CBC. The dynamic is similar to what is happening in public services. The network starves the public-affairs shows of money that is needed to do quality investigative journalism and then later cancels them because of declining popularity. Public television and radio, always an alternative to the commercialism of the private media, are being starved of resources. While the Internet could represent a counterforce to this corporatization, it too is becoming commercialized; alternative voices there may be marginalized as quickly as they have been in print and electronic media.

As politics becomes the art of the sound bite and advocacy groups are increasingly marginalized, there is less and less public space for debating political ideas. The first targets of the right were advocacy groups like the National Action Committee on the Status of Women, which were branded "special-interest groups." In the late 1980s, right-wing forces began to attack the public funding of these groups. If NAC represents women, they would say, then let women fund it. The idea, developed under Pierre Trudeau, that groups with little power should receive public funding to balance the overwhelming influence of business and other elite groups began to disappear. Of course, the money was never really the issue. At the height of its government funding in the mid-1980s, NAC received around $750,000. Even the Canadian Manufacturing Association got more public funding than that. Instead, the attacks against so-called special-interest groups were meant to undermine whatever influence they had gained over the previous few decades.

While these attacks permitted the Mulroney government to cut NAC's funding by 50 percent in 1989, the organization was sufficiently high profile in the early 1990s to recover the cuts through private fund-raising. But once NAC was hit with the double whammy of the sharp right turn in Ontario on the one hand and the racist reaction to women of colour presidents on the other, raising funds became more and more difficult. After the Charlottetown Accord campaign, NAC was also marginalized by journalists, who were convinced that they had given the organization too much visibility and therefore too much power. This backlash extended well beyond NAC, with most advocacy groups losing their visibility and authority. This combined with a ferocious attack against "union bosses" by right-wing politicians. Although such groups remain a primary vehicle for citizens' direct participation in political life, their influence and visibility has significantly declined in a period when their voices are needed more than ever.

During the same period, anger against the Mulroney government was growing across the country. The Spicer Commission, which was established in 1990 to test public opinion on constitutional issues, uncovered what Chairperson Keith Spicer referred to as "a fury in the land." Today this fury seems to have settled into resigned acceptance. Desperately needed reforms of the electoral system, which Pierre Lortie recommended in his 1991 Royal Commission on Electoral Reform and Party Financing, have withered on the vine. Although we've seen majority governments elected across the country with a minority of votes — and sometimes even fewer votes than their opponents — there is little debate about the need for a more democratic electoral system, such as proportional representation.

Now that the government of Canada is running huge surpluses instead of deficits, there is a new opening for the debate about what kind of Canada we want. The right has clearly defined its project, and it has little to do with fiscal responsibility and everything to do with greed. Now that the deficit has been eliminated, most of the braying voices of business are demanding tax cuts. So far the public isn't buying, but unless the left comes up with better proposals than simply reinstating the social programs we have lost, the overwhelming public presence of the right will once again pressure government to do what's wrong.

This was never made so obvious as in the re-election campaign of the Tories in Ontario in 1999. Mike Harris and his supporters are like the self-satisfied first-class passengers on the *Titanic*, bragging about how good things are on board the ship, unaware of the danger ahead. As a leader, Harris appeals to the worst in people. It's an "us against them" mind-set: hard-working, taxpaying citizens against welfare bums, squeegee kids, and union bosses. The polarization is deep. Men support him more than women; middle-aged people more than the young or old; high-income earners more than low. The cleavages are between those with power and those without.

The Liberal government in Ottawa, meanwhile, talks differently but is doing pretty much the same things. Prime Minister Jean Chrétien's party has shred more of the social safety net than any single government before it. The once effective unemployment insurance program is in tatters. Now covering 34 percent of unemployed people instead of 70 percent, it no longer protects the majority of workers. The repeal of the Canada Assistance Plan removed the only right to income that poor people had, and its replacement, the Canada Health and Social Transfer (CHST), gave provincial governments free rein to massively cut back on welfare payments and use federal funding for more popular health and education programs. Poor people have been left destitute, and many are now homeless.

The NDP, facing corporate and bureaucratic pressures in government and ideological and media pressure in opposition, is in the process of abandoning the basic tenets of social democracy and embracing a Tony Blair–style neo-liberalism with a human face. The rest of the broad left — as defined by social movements, the trade-union movement, and citizens' movements — has struggled mightily to resist the rapid right-wing slide. Long-time activists have retreated into their private lives because of despair over their ability to effect social change. Progressive young people who a generation ago might have been political activists move instead into the fields of culture or even small business, where they feel they can have more impact. The betrayals of governments that were supposed to be on our side — from Bob Rae's Social Contract to Glen Clark's embrace of the forest industry — have fed into the demoralization and cynicism as much as the attacks from the right have.

As a result of the strength of these movements, right-wing politics has settled on Canada much later than it did in Britain and the United States. A new youth movement is tackling the human-rights abuses of globalization both in Canada and around the world. But with no political parties expressing the alternatives these groups seek, their ability to influence public policy is limited. The one bright light has come from groups fighting international trade deals with increasing success.

The left has been caught in a rapidly deteriorating holding pattern. Ever since the loss of the free-trade fight in 1988, the left has been on the defensive, resisting attacks from the right. What has been lost as a result is the vision of an alternative. What is missing are new ideas and policies for the twenty-first century.

What we need is a society where wealth is shared; where every human being has the right not only to express an opinion but also to fully participate in public life; where every person has inherent dignity and can live free of hunger and fear; where an accident of birth does not determine one's life path; where true equality is a constant goal; where our collective responsibility for our community's well-being is as important as our private responsibility for our family's well-being. These values are still cherished by a large part of the Canadian population — the challenge is to make them real in the face of corporate globalization and greed.

This book is about alternatives. Over the past ten years, my political thinking has changed a lot. My experiences, especially as president of the National Action Committee on the Status of Women from 1990 to 1993, have led me to believe that the fuller participation of citizens in public life is the key to countering the effects of globalization. Ontario's political journey since 1990, when the NDP's Bob Rae was elected premier, has also deeply affected my ideas. Ontario moved from supporting a left-wing government that no one believed could be elected to supporting an extremely ideological right-wing government that no one believed could be elected, the latter far more successful politically than the former. I apologize in advance to readers in other parts of the country. Ontario will come up for discussion frequently in this book. But it has been a political hothouse for the past decade, and there are many lessons we can learn from it.

Globalization has severely restricted our democratic institutions, but then we had a limited view of democracy to begin with. We need a new form of democracy in the twenty-first century. Democracy in North America is not working, and the benefits of society are being hoarded by fewer and fewer people. Perhaps we need to return to democracy's roots. The Greek philosopher Aristotle defined it as a community of people dedicated to the common good. This very first theorist of democracy in the Western world understood that the democratic system could not survive except under conditions of equality.

Thomas Paine, a leader in the American independence movement and another democratic theorist, also understood this. He wrote in his essay *The Rights of Man:*

> It appears to general observation, that revolutions create genius and talents; but those events do no more than bring them forward. There exists in man [*sic*], a mass of sense lying in a dormant state, and which, unless something excites it to action, will descend with him, in that condition to the grave. As it is to the advantage of society that the whole of its faculties should be employed, the construction of government ought to be able as such to bring forward, by a quiet and regular operation, all that extent of capacity which never fails to appear in revolutions.

Democracy should be designed, argued Paine, to bring out that genius in everyday people because society would benefit tremendously from unleashing so much energy and creativity. Throughout my life, I have seen that genius expressed in people organizing for social change. In this book, I will take you on my journey of discovery and show you how I learned that the genius of ordinary people can be liberated and harnessed to create a better community, a better country, and a better world. This book is not a complete program for social transformation, but it does present some new ideas about how we can deepen democracy and develop the alternatives we need. I hope this book will stimulate debate about a new left politics that will inspire a generation to alter a path that is leading to disaster.

1

FROM ELITE TO MASS POLITICS

THE DAY THAT NAC SAID NO to the 1992 Charlottetown Accord, an amendment to the constitution, was one of the most nerve-wracking and exhilarating I've ever had. Most of my day was spent teetering on that fine line between fear and excitement. I wasn't sure what to do. There was no question in my mind that NAC should oppose the accord, which dealt with issues such as the decentralization of federal powers, aboriginal self-government, Senate reform, and Quebec's status as a distinct society. But taking a public No stance in a referendum would mean mounting a campaign. And this particular campaign was going to be a lonely one: our usual allies in the labour movement were on the Yes side. "Imagine the impact in the country if the women's movement and the labour movement joined forces to present a left-wing No," I had said to Bob White, the president of the Canadian Labour Congress (CLC). "Unfortunately, the NDP is part of the left," he answered. Although he agreed with my criticisms of the accord, he felt that his organization had to say Yes. With three NDP premiers and the aboriginal chiefs among those at the negotiating table, he believed it was the best deal we could get. "If you think we can get a better deal in the future, then lay it out for me; otherwise I think we have to support it," he explained.

With the labour movement on the other side, I was very sceptical that NAC could run the kind of campaign that would be necessary to put in a credible showing. We were accustomed to forming coalitions on most issues. We weren't used to opposing an issue all on our own, and we obviously couldn't join forces with Preston Manning's Reform Party, which was on the No side primarily because it objected to special status for Quebec. Also, NAC had never run an electoral-style campaign. Although the women's movement was becoming radicalized as our governments moved further to the right, NAC was still basically a lobby group. We had conducted cross-country campaigns during elections, but we had never tried to influence the outcome of a vote. Election campaigns for NAC were focused on getting the parties to respond to women's concerns and speak on women's issues. Campaigning to defeat a proposition in a referendum was quite a different story. I wasn't sure we could do it.

The NAC president, like the president of the CLC, is, among other things, a link between the world of the elites and the everyday world of her organization's members. Elite accommodation is the system whereby different interests are brokered in a democracy. Leaders of different interest groups present their positions to cabinet ministers or parliamentary committees and — according to the mythology, at least — the government, as a neutral body, weighs the arguments and concerns and arrives at a policy. The reality is of course more complex. The government has its own agenda, which is both ideological and political. And in a capitalist democracy, business and corporate interests have far more weight than other interests because of their economic clout (not to mention their financial backing of the two major parties). The leader of an out group, such as labour or women, must make the most noise possible to ensure that his or her voice is heard. Women's groups have an influence on this process of elite accommodation only when they show that they can mobilize public opinion. Then they may be recognized, at least for a time, as part of the elite process. We might call this elite recognition.

In these days of the ascendancy of neo-liberalism, governments and politicians are working less and less to include the out groups. Nevertheless, for any major decision to have legitimacy, it must include at least a nod to the major interests involved. The best way to illustrate this point is to look at how NAC was treated by the Mulroney government — and in particular by the lead minister, Joe Clark — in the period before the vote on the Charlottetown Accord.

Prime Minister Brian Mulroney was desperate to get some credibility for his government's constitutional proposals in the era after the failure of the Meech Lake Accord in June 1990, so he decided to call for a series of popular conferences. The Spicer Commission (also called the Citizens' Forum on Canada's Future), which held cross-country meetings later that year with Canadians to find out their concerns, had uncovered a hornet's nest of complaints, resentments, and anger. An acquaintance of mine who worked on the commission said the number-one question of participants was how to impeach the prime minister. And when a special joint committee of the House of Commons and the Senate, the Beaudoin-Dobbie Committee, travelled the country to hear proposals for constitutional change in 1991, it was mired in controversy. No one really believed that anything they said to the committee would be represented in the final proposals.

Mulroney's popular conferences in early 1992 were meant to retrieve some credibility for the process of constitutional change. Five conferences would be held in different parts of the country, each one focusing on a different aspect of the constitutional proposals. In Halifax, the forum would look at the division of powers. In Calgary, the elected Senate. In Montreal, economic union. In Toronto, minority rights. At the end, in Vancouver, a final set of proposals would be adopted. Individual Canadians could apply to attend, alongside academics, representatives of advocacy groups, unions, and business groups, and politicians. Participants were

13

chosen based on their region, gender, occupation, and area of interest. Each weekend session was organized by a different independent think-tank, which controlled the agenda and the method of organizing. The results were astonishing. The presence of ordinary citizens meant that many interests, including my own, were put to the test of direct democracy.

At the first conference, in Halifax in January 1992, NAC argued for different powers for Quebec than for the other provinces. While the rest of Canada wanted a strong federal government, Quebec wanted more provincial power. Why can't we do both? we asked. Immediately, the government, which had identified people's willingness to accommodate Quebec as the key to the whole constitutional process, saw me as an ally. In the late 1980s, the media had erroneously written that NAC opposed Meech Lake because it gave Quebec too much power, so our position in favour of distinct society and asymmetrical federalism was news. After years of being snubbed by the Mulroney Tories, we were suddenly included. Much to our surprise, we won over the Halifax conference to our position on Quebec, and then the media started to pay attention. We were players.

But our new status was not to last. As soon as the premiers took over the constitutional negotiations in March 1992, rejecting not only asymmetrical federalism but also the proposal to elect the Senate by proportional representation (which had been embraced by Beaudoin-Dobbie in its final report), NAC was on the outs again. Aboriginal groups, excluding the Native Women's Association, were invited to take part in the closed-door negotiations leading up to the Charlottetown Accord (these took place in various locations across the country from March to August), but women's groups, despite having played a key role at every stage of constitutional change, were not.

After intensive lobbying, we got the provincial premiers to agree to see us in a side meeting in Ottawa, but few of them showed up and their attitude towards us was one of bare tolerance. After we realized that almost everything we had fought for at the conferences was being rejected by the premiers, we organized a demonstration during the final meeting in Charlottetown in August 1992. By this time, everyone from the premiers to the national media saw us as a major annoyance. I remember journalists rolling their eyes as I went up to the mike at those famous organized scrums outside the meeting rooms.

But we weren't dead yet. In the lobby of the conference centre in Charlottetown, about one hundred local activists and a few national women's leaders confronted the premiers about gender parity in the Senate and protection in the Charter of Rights and Freedoms for aboriginal women. In public, Ontario's Bob Rae told me that while he and his fellow premiers had opted for regional elections over proportional representation (PR) as a way of choosing the Senate, his government would incorporate gender parity on a provincial level. Then Nova Scotia also committed to gender parity, and B.C. and Saskatchewan said they would consider it. Suddenly we were players again, at least from the point of view of the media.

Gender parity in the Senate had never been a major issue for NAC. We were more concerned with the possibility that provinces might win the right to opt out on social programs, which we thought would scupper any chance of a national childcare program; the lack of charter protection for aboriginal women; and the weakening of the rights of women and racial minorities in comparison to other groups listed in the Charlottetown Accord's so-called Canada Clause, which we called a hierarchy of rights. We came up with the idea of gender parity during the constitutional discussions because it seemed like a good idea at the time. If we were really to have a so-called Triple-E Senate (elected, effective, and equal), then surely that equality should mean more than just equality for the provinces. If a new elected institution was to be established, we wanted women to play a major role in it.

At the second Calgary conference at the end of January, NAC had made a compromise with the Triple-E proponents to support election of the Senate by PR. The Triple-E people were against gender parity but argued that PR would result in a higher number of women being elected. In addition, PR as a system of election in the Senate would open the door to similar electoral reforms in the House of Commons. NAC made an alliance with the Triple-E people at Calgary, and together we won the conference to a proposal for a Triple-E Senate elected by proportional representation. Indeed, some of our advisers, such as the pioneer feminist Doris Anderson, felt that we should have been arguing for PR from the beginning. But when the premiers arrogantly rejected the demand for PR, we went back to gender parity, which was a simpler idea. Not surprisingly, it was this demand that most captured the imagination of women in government and in the political parties.

We had assumed that the positions adopted by the conferences would be seriously considered by the premiers when they began the constitutional negotiations in earnest. We were wrong. Once the premiers and the aboriginal leaders actually got to the table, it was their interests that dominated. They basically ignored what had gone before. NAC had no choice but to go back to protest politics.

It is movement in the other direction, from protest politics to elite recognition, that best describes the path of advocacy groups in a liberal democracy. To get enough power to be included, even for a time, in the process of elite accommodation an advocacy group has to demonstrate its ability to affect public opinion, attract media attention, or disrupt politics as usual. When journalists say to me that demonstrations and rallies are a throwback to the 1960s, what they are really saying is that media savvy and the politics of spin are more important. What they don't recognize is that however good the spin, groups without institutional or economic power have to demonstrate political might either by getting people in power to act or by mobilizing people without power in the streets, on the phones, and through virtual or actual mail. We now found ourselves back at this level.

Groups like NAC and the Canadian Labour Congress (CLC) are meant to represent the views of ordinary citizens, and they often do. In Ekos Research's 1998 study *Rethinking Government,* 66 percent of general respondents said they had a lot of confidence in non-profit and voluntary organizations; only 28 percent expressed such confidence in the government. Compare that with the response of the elite decision-makers, 48 percent of whom said they had a lot of confidence in government.

The problem with the out groups is that often their leaders are co-opted. Indeed, one criticism of NAC has focused on its refusal to become a permanent part of the elite. Once there were women in cabinet, we were expected to meet with the ministers, hope they would bring our concerns to the table, and wait politely for them to do so. Every time NAC organized a protest that went beyond the mildest of tactics, we would lose credibility with Parliament Hill reporters, who wanted us to follow the rules. I remember when David Vienneau of the *Toronto Star,* usually one of the most sympathetic reporters on the Hill, described as "bizarre" a protest that saw NAC women pounding on the doors of the House of Commons, which had been shut in our faces.

Because of NAC's structure as a federation of women's groups, its presidents are always under pressure from their member organizations to maintain a grass-roots approach to politics. At the executive board meeting where NAC was to affirm its position on the Charlottetown Accord, the constitutional committee, which included me, decided to put forward three options without any recommendation. Our hope was that the other members of NAC, when forced to make their own choice, would be thorough in weighing the options.

We had already decided that we could not support the accord unconditionally. Our options then became to say Yes and hold our noses like the CLC was doing; to support it if the premiers and the federal government amended the Canada Clause to ensure no hierarchy of rights and allowed the Charter of Rights and Freedoms to apply to aboriginal self-government; or to say No and campaign against the accord.

The change in composition of NAC to include previously marginalized women had altered the entire manner in which we examined issues. Certainly we were still concerned about how our role would play in the media and whether we would gain or lose credibility. But the discussion that day did not focus on those issues. Instead, woman after woman said she believed that the accord would damage the interests of women, especially aboriginal women; weaken our social programs; and create a new elected institution that, while ostensibly equal and effective, would be just as unrepresentative as the ones we already had.

In the end, almost every woman spoke in favour of the No campaign. We wanted to be so certain that this was a carefully considered position, however, that one of our committee members who most supported the No side argued against her own position. I was astonished by the passion in the room, as well as by the antagonism towards the accord that was voiced not only by NAC executive members but also by women and men that they knew, including aboriginal women and women from Quebec. They all felt that support for the accord in their communities was weak.

I almost couldn't believe it. In the world of elite politics from which I had just come, everyone supported the accord. Members of the racist, right-wing, anti-Quebec Reform Party opposed it, of course, but no one expected anything better from them. Almost everyone else was falling in line. Maybe it wasn't the best deal, they said, but it does support self-government and an elected Senate, and it opposes big business' desire for an economic union that would have created a race to the bottom among the provinces. And of course, the prime minister had just accused anyone who opposed the deal of being a traitor. You had to be pretty sure of your position if you were in the No camp.

Later in the afternoon of September 13, we held a press conference. Even on a Sunday afternoon, the media were there in force. NAC's vice-president, Shelagh Day, had come up with a good line: "We tried to hold our noses and vote Yes, but we choked." NAC Says No was our campaign slogan, and it was on front pages across the country the next day. Even at the height of the abortion struggle, I never experienced a day like the one after NAC said No. Not only was I interviewed by every media outlet in the country, but every politician who had ever been an ally of NAC's, from Bob Rae to Joe Clark to Audrey McLaughlin, denounced us. In the world of elite politics, everyone attacked NAC and accused us of defending only a narrow interest.

While I was at my Toronto apartment with Shelagh Day trying to cover the media calls on my two phone lines, the NAC office was swamped with a tidal wave of support from the public. On the day after we came out against the accord, 80 percent of the calls were positive. The day after that, 90 percent of the calls were positive, and on the third day almost every call was positive. It remained that way for the rest of the campaign. Never had I experienced such a total disconnect between the worlds of elite and mass politics. As the person on the NAC executive who lived most in the world of elite politics, I was the one who was the most nervous about the organization's decision. But my concerns had turned out to be unfounded. My board members were much closer to their communities, in this case, than the elected politicians were.

The night before NAC was to decide its position on the Charlottetown Accord, Joe Clark phoned me to try to convince me not to join the No side. Despite having ignored our issues for all the months of the premiers' meetings, he was suddenly concerned about what our influence might be in a referendum. At that time, his major worry was British Columbia. Polls there were already indicating that the accord could be in trouble. And in a poll taken in Ontario a few days after NAC said No, support for the Yes side had fallen to 41 percent from 57 percent only two weeks earlier.

Clark's attitude towards me on the phone was rather patronizing. There are big stakes here, he seemed to be saying, the unity of the country, self-government for aboriginal people . . . Surely you won't put that into jeopardy for your petty concerns? Our petty concerns, I countered, were protection of social programs and aboriginal women, as well as the advancement of political equality for women. These, Clark said the next day in the media, were narrow interests.

If we had been focusing on narrow self-interest, we probably would have accepted Clark's rather desperate last-minute offer to try to improve the language in the Canada Clause. But NAC had decided to oppose the accord because our members thought it was bad for women and bad for the country, not because it was bad for NAC member groups. Still, saying No was a very risky strategy for the organization.

During this debate, the world of elite accommodation politics gave way to the world of mass politics. The problem in this particular case was that almost all the elites were on one side. The usual divisions along class and regional lines had disappeared under the pressure of "keeping the country together." NAC and Reform each in its own way represented the wishes of the people, but neither group was strong enough at the time to win a seat at the negotiating table. There was no other option for us than to defeat the accord unconditionally, with no alternative.

Because he was accepting the rules of elite accommodation, Bob White had probably made the correct decision when he opted to support the accord. The economic union pushed for by the business elite had been eliminated, giving labour a major victory. And aboriginal self-government was a major step forward for those who supported aboriginal rights. But for NAC, representing the interests of women, the failure of the accord to include self-government in the Charter of Rights and Freedoms put hard-earned aboriginal women's rights in jeopardy; the opt-out on social programs was at least as important as the economic union; and the wording of the Canada Clause seemed to put everything we had fought for in the charter into jeopardy. It's not that the CLC leaders were unconcerned with these issues, of course, but that their major concerns lay elsewhere.

I continue to believe that if the labour movement had joined NAC in a progressive No campaign, we might have been able to force a couple of key changes. Of course, Bob White probably believes that if NAC had joined his principled Yes campaign, we would now be much further ahead on both aboriginal self-government and the Quebec issue. Maybe he is right. Either way, the debate over the Charlottetown Accord showed how important it is for the fullest flowering of democracy that the mass and elite planes of politics feed each other. Most politicians understand that if these planes become too separated, conflict, chaos, and revolution will follow. That is why groups like NAC and the CLC sometimes achieve elite recognition. But what we have never explored is what creative potential lies in ensuring more and deeper interaction between these levels.

I used to believe that the essence of democracy was the clash of ideas and interests. From both the conflict and the coming together of diverse ideas and interests, democracy allows for a creative re-invention of society to meet at least some of the needs of not only the majority but also excluded minorities of various types. It is this process that has kept capitalism alive so long after it should have been jettisoned into the dustbin of history.

There is, however, another plane of democracy, one just as important: the bottom-up, vertical plane that travels from the ordinary citizen to the community, to advocacy groups, to the government. In Western democracies today, this plane is covered mostly by opinion polls and elections every four or five years. Since the 1970s, advocacy groups have been a primary vehicle for bringing the views and interests of ordinary people into the political arena. In the past few years, however, such groups have been increasingly marginalized. Right-wing governments like Ontario's don't even pretend to include such groups in decision making. They are in the process of destroying the social contract that these groups helped create; it is essential, therefore, for them to remove any legitimacy such groups have to speak for the public interest. It is no accident that the first goal of right-wing groups like the Reform Party and the Fraser Institute was to discredit advocacy groups like NAC. Today only the corporate elite is assumed to speak for the public interest. Other groups are branded "special interest" and relegated to society's margins.

Supporters of the process of elite accommodation, like the *Globe and Mail* columnist Jeffrey Simpson, decry the influence of advocacy groups but also criticize governing by opinion poll and the direct democracy of referendum. Right-wing populists like Reform Party members support forms of direct democracy while maintaining policies to promote the interests of the economic elite. As advocacy groups lose their credibility, politicians rely more and more on opinion polls to determine their priorities. Barracuda political strategists like President Bill Clinton's James Carvelle or Mike Harris's Tom Long, along with highly sophisticated spin doctors like the consultants of the Earnscliffe Group in Ottawa, are building an industry on politics as spin. Getting the media to shape public opinion by reporting the results of instant polling is becoming a substitute for elite recognition of advocacy leaders.

While this may appear more democratic, it is not. For one thing, opinion polls, especially the quick and dirty ones that so many members of the media are fond of using, are constructed in the image of the country's power elite. During the dark days of the shift to the right in the mid-1990s, for example, opinion polls never mentioned poverty as an issue. They might have mentioned children's poverty or the plight of the working poor, but not poverty or homelessness in general. As municipalities made homelessness more of a concern, however, the public framing of the poverty issue changed. In addition to child poverty, homelessness — and its effects on nice, middle-class communities — became the top-of-mind issue as the 1990s drew to a close.

Another problem with polls is that people's opinions are not often well considered or well informed. When someone phones you at home as you are cooking dinner and asks whether you think the government should prioritize social spending or debt reduction

— or even more ridiculously, whether your opinion of the prime minister went up or down after last night's debate — it is unlikely that your answer will reflect a well-considered opinion. In fact, more and more people are refusing even to answer opinion polls, which makes their results even more suspect. Opinion polls are useful in judging the horse race of elections and can be useful in judging trends over time, but they are no substitute for the difficult process of brokering different interests.

The problem with elite accommodation, meanwhile, is that the opinions of the elites too often do not reflect the opinions of most citizens. Ekos Research Associates, in a 1994 study called *Rethinking Government,* compared the opinions of a random sample of 2,400 Canadians with those of top government and corporate decision-makers. When they were asked what the values for the federal government should be, the ordinary Canadians prioritized freedom, a clean environment, a healthy population, integrity, and individual rights. The elite decision-makers prioritized competitiveness, integrity, minimal government, thriftiness, and excellence. Competitiveness was ranked twentieth on the people's list and minimal government came in last, at number twenty-two.

The experience of the Charlottetown referendum changed my ideas about democracy. As I travelled from coast to coast, speaking at hundreds of meetings and on dozens of talk shows, I found an informed and articulate population. I may not always have agreed with people's views, but it was clear that they had carefully thought out what they were saying. Many people would come to meetings with a marked up copy of the accord and written questions to ask the participants, who usually represented the two sides. I had never felt such intense political participation. Because people knew that they had a direct vote on the outcome, they got more involved. They listened to and watched the debate, came to meetings, called talk shows, and discussed the issues among themselves. Since the differences didn't fall along the usual left-right spectrum, people had to decide for themselves what they thought. They couldn't just follow the person they most trusted politically, whether that person was Bob White or Preston Manning.

Although my side won the referendum, I felt terribly depressed, even in the midst of the media flurry. After watching, on the night of October 26, the reaction of the premiers on the huge TV screens at the CBC's referendum headquarters, I knew that the defeat of the Charlottetown Accord would have little positive impact. No one on the No side was close enough to the corridors of power to bring the popular message to the table where decisions are made. We had slowed them down, but that was all. And ironically, the main impact, as it later turned out, was to make the Reform Party a major force in the country and reduce the NDP to irrelevance.

The tremendous cynicism about politics that infects North Americans is almost entirely based on the feeling that no matter what the people think, politicians will do what they like. In our system, politicians are meant to represent the interests of the average elector. Their lives in the capital, whether it's Ottawa or a provincial capital, are far removed from the lives of their constituents. The day-to-day pressures come from bureaucrats, lobbyists, and the media, not from the people they are supposed to serve. Even politicians who remain true to their constituents are blocked at every turn by the hierarchical structure of a political system that gives all the power to party leaders, cabinet ministers, and their staffs.

Polls are a superficial and distorted indication of popular opinion, and elections are spaced too far apart to have enough impact. Advocacy groups are an essential element in bringing the voice of the people into the corridors of power, but they are too easily marginalized in times when that voice is most needed.

The missing element is the informed participation of the average person. We need to transform our system, preserving what works best and introducing a strong dose of direct democracy, to enable the participation of ordinary citizens who can bring the needs, interests, and experiences of their communities into the political arena.

2

ACTIVE CITIZENSHIP

I HAD HEARD ABOUT LULA DA SILVA FOR YEARS, but my first
contact with him — at a breakfast sponsored by the United
Steelworkers of America in November 1997 — was disappointing.
There he was on the edges of the crowd that had come together
that morning to meet him. He didn't speak English or French, so
most could not converse with him without assistance, but even in
his physical manner he downplayed his own importance. Unlike
our politicians, he did nothing to draw attention to himself.

It wasn't until later that evening — at a public meeting I was
chairing in downtown Toronto — that I got a taste of the Lula da
Silva who attracts tens of thousands of Brazilians to rallies just to
catch a glimpse of the socialist steelworker who had almost become
president. He spoke in Portuguese, but even in translation his passion filled the room. In simple but profound language he explained
how the Workers Party (PT) in Brazil was seeking an alternative to
the politics of corporate globalization. His charisma was in the promotion of his ideas, not in self-promotion.

The heart of his argument was that people of the world need to
develop a new vision of a fairer society. The democratic participation

of people in that society, he said, has to be the centre of that new vision. He calls this vision social citizenship, a new kind of democracy.

"Do we have democracy only to have the right to cry out in hunger?" he asked. What was the meaning of political democracy in Brazil, he demanded, if so much of the population was struggling just to survive? In a developing country like Brazil, where so many live in poverty, these simple questions proved to have revolutionary implications. In the cities and regions where the PT is in power, they have put their ideas into practice by involving ordinary citizens in the decisions that affect their lives.

As I listened to Lula talk, I thought of my own country. In Canada, it seems that democracy means less and less as cynicism towards politicians grows. The social movements of my youth have turned into pale shadows of themselves, and the gap between rich and poor grows ever wider, pushing elite experience further and further from the life of most people. Profound decisions affecting our lives are made in secret by international bureaucrats and multinational corporations. Do we have democracy, I wondered, just to cry out our alienation from the political process?

That night, Lula said that members of the PT did not have a road map to this new kind of democracy, but that they were learning from their experiences as they went. "Where we are in power, we turn neo-liberalism on its head. That's our starting point," he explained. "We start from the needs of the people, not the needs of capital."

So what is it like when Lula's PT puts its ideas into practice? In Brazil's Gaucho country, municipalities are taking part in what is called a participatory budget (OP). In Pôrto Alegre, a city of one million, ordinary citizens actually decide on their municipality's priorities through the OP. Every year, citizens are elected to serve alongside city councillors in sixteen geographically and socially distinct sectors. In March and April, in the early stages of the OP, a progress report on decisions made the previous year is presented and debated by the citizen forums in each sector. The forums are open and advertised. Anyone in the region can attend, and each person who attends gets one vote. The mayor's office, which organizes the process, encourages poor people to attend by using neighbourhood associations to mobilize them. Every person gets an information booklet and a financial report that explains every major expenditure.

The budget process starts in March, with general assemblies in each region. Five to seven hundred people attend each forum. The forums then elect two representatives and two alternates; these people serve unpaid for one year only on the OP council. Each one of the sixteen citizen assemblies, in addition to electing representatives for the city-wide budget council, decides what service and spending priorities it wants to see in the coming year. This is done in April and May through a series of smaller meetings organized by the elected delegates. The mayor and members of his staff attend only two meetings, one at the beginning and one at the end of the process. The proposals from all the forums are forwarded to the municipal council, and at the same time, the delegates to the city-wide budget council attend training sessions on municipal finance. A draft budget, which is based on the initial proposals from the regional and sectoral assemblies, goes back and forth between municipal bureaucrats and the OP council, and then finally is sent to the mayor and the municipal council, which has the sole authority to actually adopt the budget.

By this point in the process, we are in mid-July. The legal force of universal suffrage and representative democracy, in the persons of the thirty-three traditionally elected municipal councillors, meets with the grass-roots power of direct democracy, embodied in the forty or so OP councillors (and, by extension, in the hundreds of delegates who participated in the regional and sectoral forums and the 20,000 citizens who took an active part in the various stages of the OP). It is the OP that, between October and December, debates, discusses, and amends the plan for the new year. The municipal council has the final say, but it is understood that it will make only minor changes to the OP proposal.

I met Raul Ponte, the mayor of Pôrto Alegre, in Toronto in the summer of 1999. A solidarity group in Montreal had brought him to Canada to share the experience of the participatory budget with activists here. "When we were elected in 1988," said Ponte, "we had a commitment to govern through popular councils, but no experience in how to do it." As with many governments, they found that they had no money to accomplish their goals. One hundred percent of tax money was going out in expenditures. "We brought together all the existing groups in each region — unions and various neighbourhood groups — and asked them what to do. At first, people thought it was a trick."

Instead of decrying the previous administration and using that as an excuse to break election promises, the PT invited these groups to lobby for a more progressive tax system. The groups told the PT that there was a lot of corruption in the municipal government that could be corrected. The next year, around 3,000 people attended the open meetings; last year 20,000 attended.

"People come because they know they will really influence decision making," Ponte explained. "When we ran in 1988, we placed public transportation as the number-one issue, but people told us that we were wrong. While transportation was important, other issues were much more important. A top issue was childcare centres in the early days. In our second term, we had no schools for the 0 to 6 age group. Over three years, we went from one childcare centre to 120. We didn't have enough money to set up the day-care centres as municipal services, so community centres offered to run the services. This made them affordable. Workers got paid less than they would have in municipal services, but there were many new jobs created that we couldn't have afforded to create through the municipality." The mayor had to drop his traditional left insistence on the municipality providing all public services and instead make a compromise that would better serve his citizens.

Not everyone on the city council is comfortable with this process. In fact, half of the councillors voted to stop the participatory budget, believing it interferes with their right to govern.

28

Today, of the thirty-three members of city council, only fourteen are from the PT. "Old-style politicians don't like the idea that people themselves are making the decisions," says Ponte. But the people of Pôrto Alegre like it so much that they have re-elected the PT for three terms over eleven years; last year the PT was elected to the state government as well.

"The PT sees this as a demonstration project," explains Ponte. "When people themselves make the decisions, they decide the opposite of the neo-liberals." The participatory budget has also led workers to struggle for more decision-making power in their work-places, and it has created tremendous solidarity in neighbourhoods. Now that the PT forms the government in Brazil's southernmost state, with its population of 10 million, it will have an opportunity to design a participatory system on a much larger scale.

What is so exciting about this participatory budget is the inter-action of active citizens, elected politicians, and career officials. Instead of playing an advisory role, as do many citizen bodies in our political system, the regional and sectoral assemblies actually discuss and debate budget priorities. In my neighbourhood of Toronto, for example, we might decide that a new school is more important than improvements to the highway. In other words, those living and working in the community would decide on the priorities that directly affected their lives. Community interest, not party politics or personal gain, becomes the centre of the decision-making process. More important, instead of complaining about the decisions someone else is making on my behalf, I can become a sig-nificant participant in the process for a year or two without giving up my job and beginning a career in politics. On the contrary, it is my day-to-day experiences in the community that best qualify me for participation in deciding on the priorities for my community.

Of course, popular assemblies alone are not enough. Even if, in my neighbourhood, our citizens' assembly decided on the school, perhaps one is needed even more desperately in the next region. The overall municipal council has to decide how much money to devote to each project. If citizens are involved only at the neighbourhood level, then the real decisions will still be left to professional politicians and bureaucrats. In the OP system, electing delegates from the assemblies to a city-wide budget council ensures that direct democratic input continues throughout the entire process. The OP system also recognizes that no matter how open and welcoming a direct democracy is, it will always involve a small minority of citizens. The largest number of citizens are thus able to participate in the usual fashion of representative democracy. The OP is an example of how direct democracy and representative democracy can work together.

Another fascinating feature of the participatory budget is that most of the delegates who get involved in this exercise are the people who need the municipal services the most: the poor and the working class. Indeed, 50 percent of the participants are women. In most political systems, it is professionals such as teachers and lawyers who are most likely to get involved, but in Gaucho country it is the ordinary people, some of whom may even be illiterate, who participate most fully. What an interesting way to counter the natural elitism of the system of representative democracy.

Hugo Chavez, who was elected president of Venezuela in December 1998, is also following the path of participatory democracy. Chavez's program attracted 57 percent of the vote in a country where the gap between rich and poor is a virtual chasm. Even though the country has made $300 billion from petroleum sales over the past twenty-five years, half of its population lives in poverty. In an October 1999 interview, Chavez told *Le Monde diplomatique*: "Democracy isn't just a matter of political equality. It's also and especially about social, economic and cultural equality. . . . I want to be the poor people's president, but we must learn from the failure of other revolutions which, while they claimed to have those aims, either betrayed them or pursued them but did away with democracy in the process. . . . What we are trying to do is move from a representative democracy — and there's not necessarily anything wrong with that — to a participative one; one in which the people are more fully involved at all levels of the power structure, so that they can fight any violation of human rights more effectively."

In Canada, I have participated in a similar system only once, and that was during the cross-country forums on the Charlottetown Accord that I discussed in the previous chapter. Before the forums, I was sceptical not only about whether the government would permit a genuinely democratic process but also about the wisdom of ordinary citizens. I figured that most of them would be virulently anti-Quebec, and that that would prevent any real solutions from emerging. I was wrong on both counts. The ordinary citizens were astonishing. They listened carefully to everyone and expressed their concerns, including their frustration over how much Quebec had got in the past. In one workshop, a woman from New Brunswick almost hit me at the end of the first day. She was so angry at Quebec and at my insistence that we had to have a solution that accommodated the province's needs. But by the end of the second day, she had totally changed her views.

Eventually, the Halifax conference voted in favour of asymmetrical federalism, and it was again confirmed at the final conference in Vancouver. Unfortunately, it was rejected by the powers that be as unsellable. Having presented it to Canadians from coast to coast, I knew that this idea, which I still think is the best solution to the Quebec-Canada impasse, was anything but unsellable. It could not be sold to the people in power only because it would mean that some of them would lose a little authority. This illustrates one reason why participatory democracy is so important: voting every four or five years does not exert enough pressure on elected politicians to counter the corruption of power.

I first started thinking about participatory democracy during a 1991 conference on democratic administration that was organized by York University's political science department under the leadership of Leo Panitch. Panitch had been arguing, ever since the NDP's unexpected Ontario election victory the year before, that the most important thing the government could do was democratize the state, involving citizens at every level of policy making and policy implementation. Legislation can easily be turned over, he said. The only change that would make a lasting difference would be to develop a more direct relationship with the people. At the time, I thought the ideas interesting but not very convincing. Then I watched with horror as Bob Rae's government caved in to corporate pressure on everything from auto insurance to the deficit and never once looked to the people to mobilize support, and with even greater horror as a subsequent right-wing government overturned in the wink of an eye most of what the NDP did accomplish. Now I realize the wisdom of the York conference, and in particular of Hilary Wainright, a British socialist-feminist academic and activist whom I first met at the conference. In the coming pages, I will refer frequently to the ideas presented at the conference, which are now in book form.

Wainright talked about a new kind of knowledge based not on expertise but on human experience. The social movements of the 1960s, she said, were the first to value and develop such knowledge. For example, feminist consciousness-raising groups grew out of women's experiences and then moved to develop demands based on women's expression of that experience. Today, women's willingness to share their personal problems has led to a critique of existing government programs and services and the development of alternatives, such as rape-crisis centres, day-care centres, and women's centres.

"A distinctive feature of these [social] movements is their stress on the legitimacy of the insights, skills, even feelings of their members as an essential contribution to any adequate knowledge of social needs and solutions," wrote Wainright in *A Different Kind of State? Popular Power and Democratic Administration*, the book based on the conference. "The idea of knowledge as practical as well as theoretical . . . leads to strategies for transformation that no longer envisage the state as an external engineer but as the potential source of a democratic and egalitarian framework and provider of public support and protection for a variety of forms of popular self-government. In terms of traditional debates about democracy, such an approach would imply a combination of participatory and representative forms."

It is odd that I was so resistant to Wainright's ideas at that 1991 conference. Participatory democracy was one of the central features of both the New Left in the 1960s, which is where I had my first political experiences, and the women's movement, which is where my political vision matured. The 1962 Port Huron Declaration of the Students for a Democratic Society became the manifesto of a new generation of political radicals — obviously it was written before second-wave feminism got going — and it read, in part:

> We would replace power rooted in possession, privilege, or circumstance by power and uniqueness rooted in love, reflectiveness, reason, and creativity. As a social system we seek the establishment of a democracy of individual participation, governed by two central aims: that the individual share in those social decisions determining the quality and direction of his life; that society be organized to encourage independence in men and provide the media for their common participation. . . .
> In a participatory democracy, the political life would be based in several root principles: that decision-making of basic social consequence be carried on by public groupings; that politics be seen positively, as the art of collectively creating an acceptable pattern of social relations; . . . that politics has the function of bringing people out of isolation and into community, thus being a necessary, though not sufficient, means of finding meaning in personal life; . . . that the political order should serve to clarify problems in a way instrumental to their solution; it should provide outlets for the expression of personal grievance and aspiration; opposing views should be organized so as to illuminate choices and facilitate the attainment of goals; channels should be commonly available to relate

men to knowledge and to power so that private problems — from bad recreation facilities to personal alienation — are formulated as general issues.

Contained in that declaration were the seeds of a new idea that emerged from ancient origins. The original concept behind democracy was that all citizens would participate fully in the decisions affecting their lives. Through its idealism, the New Left wanted to return to democracy as it was conceived in ancient Greece and in the American Revolution.

The New Left was rich in idealism but poor in the knowledge of how to challenge the state effectively to bring about change. The ideals of participatory democracy never got much further than the campus, where students began to participate in the ruling institutions of the university for the first time. When the New Left fell apart, many of us turned to the ideas of the old left, hoping to bring with us our passion for participatory democracy. But these New Left notions went out the window in favour of the most extraordinary and arrogant form of elitism, vanguardism, which held that a small cadre of revolutionaries would develop the theories of change that the masses would eventually embrace. It was left to the women's movement to take up and extend the meaning of participatory democracy.

When I began to become active in the women's movement in 1980, I found the nature of democracy inside many of its organizations very frustrating. For a long time, the women's movement wanted to turn patriarchy on its head and have flat organizations with no recognized leaders and a process of consensus decision making. This often led to endless discussion without conclusion. And as women of colour later pointed out, the flat structure and consensus politics often masked the real leadership in the group, and therefore prevented accountability. But whatever its shortcomings, the women's movement further developed the ideas of participatory democracy as they were first put forward by the New

Left, and did this by recognizing the wisdom of everyday experience. In the early days of feminism, women knew that the world in which they lived was different from the world portrayed in male-dominated politics, media, and culture. Over time, the situation that Betty Friedan called "the problem with no name" became articulated through the exploration of individual women's experiences. To this day, feminist academics almost always include interviews with individuals as part of their work, proof that the feminist vision of knowledge is so different from the expert-based knowledge that dominates our democratic process.

Perhaps the most instructive experience of the women's movement was the process of developing alternative services. As women discovered what they needed, they found that the state was not providing those services, and so they organized themselves to provide them. Rape-crisis centres, transition houses, women's centres, day-care centres — all were organized as collectives, with the users and the workers co-operating in decisions. These services were special in a number of ways: they rejected the hierarchical command model of the public service; they included both users and workers; they valued women's day-to-day experience much more than theoretical or professional expertise; and perhaps most important, they empowered their participants. In short, these services were developed in a way that gave women the space to develop their ability to supply what was missing in their lives and in society as a whole. By identifying their own needs, developing the resources to address those needs, and organizing the resulting services, women also found the power to effect change inside themselves.

One of the most obvious differences between men and women can be seen in the way that most men are able to take up public space. Whether in a meeting, on a radio talk show, in a classroom, or in the political arena, men will almost always talk more and take command more often than women. In her book *A Room of One's Own*, Virginia Woolf puts it this way: "Women have served all these centuries as looking-glasses possessing the magic and delicious power of reflecting the figure of man at twice its natural size." This, in part, explains why so few women, even when economic inequalities are reduced, take the stage in public life.

Feminists used to believe that once barriers to access in the workplace and in politics were removed, women would take an equal place beside men in public life. But in her recent book *Arguments for a New Left*, Hilary Wainright explains that in addition to economic independence, there needs to be a conscious valuing of women's public action to ensure their full participation in political life at every level. That's why women established women-only groups at first. With men in the same group, it was impossible for women to find the female path to public action. Only in women's groups can women find their own reflection. Even today, I find that in mixed groups, women's voices, with some exceptions, are less valued. This holds doubly true for minorities.

My time in NAC made me realize that a more collective process where all voices are heard and a diversity of experience is brought to bear on a problem produces a much richer form of democracy than the top-down version favoured by modern governments. In NAC it was only when we adopted formal affirmative action and made one or two decisions that publicly supported the demands of women of colour that these women started to fully participate. The organization had to open up the space and demonstrate that it valued the public action of women of colour. Power is not given; it must be taken. But it can also be shared. This is the essence of participatory democracy.

Hilary Wainright participated in one of the most important exercises in participatory democracy in the developed world. Between 1982 and 1986, the left of the British Labour Party, under the leadership of Ken Livingston, was elected to the Greater London Council (GLC). The GLC's entry into participatory democracy was born of necessity. In order to carry out a radical agenda on a municipal level in the face of the extremely right-wing government of Margaret Thatcher at the national level, they needed the active participation of community groups. As Wainright describes it in *Arguments for a New Left*, "The left-wing councillors leading the GLC had an acute sense of the limits of knowledge that could be centralized through themselves and the officers of County Hall. . . . Out of [a] combination of political commitments from elected politicians and pressure from groups of Londoners, the GLC developed mechanisms in an ad hoc way, which made public and sometimes effective a wealth of practical knowledge ignored by the market and the conventional state alike."

A number of strategies were employed. For the first time in British history, the GLC funded groups working for social and economic change, not just those providing services. In exchange for funding, these groups elected representatives to council committees to feed back their ideas and strategies. This was a big step for the GLC, which previously had believed that the state had the wisdom to provide what was necessary for its citizens. All you needed was the right people in political leadership. The GLC politicians now delegated some of their power to citizens' groups. They lost some political control, but what they gained in terms of new knowledge and political support was invaluable.

"Representative democracy assumes that the crucial element in democracy is the expression of opinion, while the implementation of the decision is left to the experts," explains Wainright. "Once this assumption is questioned, democracy becomes more complex. Democracy becomes concerned with the process by which decisions are implemented, as well as [with] the competition of opinions and programs regarding those decisions."

Wainright argues that we must recognize the limitations of all governments, whether left-wing or right, in the area of social policy. Only when these limitations have been acknowledged will we be able to take advantage of non-traditional forms of knowledge and different sources of power.

The dream of democracy was never just to see the expression of public opinion through polls and voting — it was to see the full participation of citizens in public life. Now, at the turn of the century, citizens have never been more able to fully participate in social and political life. Indeed, in the twentieth century the ability of the average citizen to participate in the democratic process grew exponentially. Canada's per capita GNP went from $3,000 in 1890 to $19,200 in 1995. U.S. high-school enrolment climbed from 519,000 in 1890 to 17 million in 1995. Post-secondary enrolment in the United States shot up from 238,000 in 1890 to 14 million in 1995. The Canadian work week shrank from 57 hours in 1890 to 39 hours in 1994. With such dramatic shifts towards equality, why do we still have the same system of democracy? Technology gives us tools for direct democratic participation that Aristotle and Payne could not even dream of. Yet instead of moving towards greater citizen participation in public life, we are privatizing public space more and more.

During Brian Mulroney's reign, democracy itself became a major issue in Canada. The Spicer Commission, in its 1991 interim report, stated:

> Overwhelmingly, participants have told us that they have lost faith in the political system and its leadership. Anger, disillusion and a desire for fundamental change [are] very often the first issue[s] raised in discussion groups and usually produce unanimous agreement. . . . Canadians are telling us that their leaders must understand and accept their vision of the country — that their leaders must be governed by the wishes of the people and not the other way around.

Unfortunately, it was the right wing that responded to this deep desire for a more democratic society. Just as the progressive organizations once did, neo-conservatives criticized the social engineering welfare state for its patronizing "father knows best" attitude towards its citizens.

In four years of debating right-wingers as host of the CBC Newsworld show "Face Off," I never had a more unpleasant experience than when I weighed in against David Frum at Massey College in Toronto in the spring of 1997. I suppose Frum's residency in Washington, D.C., has given him that nasty edge that ideologues living in Canada manage to avoid. Within three minutes of starting his presentation, Frum had alienated all but his most ardent followers. With a turn of phrase, he dismissed both feminism and environmentalism. But he saved his best vitriol for socialism.

"Socialism is discredited," he claimed. "No one is a socialist any more, not even Judy Rebick." It was obvious he hadn't bothered to look into my views. Then he said something with which I partly agreed, which is most unfortunate in such a polarized debate. "The left used to have big ideas. Collective ownership of the means of production was a big idea. It was wrong, but it was a big idea," he proclaimed. "Now the left has only small ideas. They behave like the survivors of the destruction of an ancient civilization, keeping old habits when the civilization is long gone."

I had to grudgingly concur. In giving up on the collective ownership of the means of production or on nationalization of the heights of the economy (depending on whether you are a Marxist or a social democrat), the left has given up on its vision of a transformed society. Unfortunately, the problem was never the left's economic vision, which still makes sense. The problem was its political vision, and most especially its organizational reality.

The idea of socialism is that more wealth should be collectively owned, usually through the state, and that privately accumulated wealth should, at least in part, be redistributed to ensure that everyone has a decent standard of living. The abiding maxim of socialists is Marx's "From each according to his abilities, to each according to his need." Capitalism, as an economic system, is inherently unjust. When self-interest is the driving force in a society, those with the most access to wealth and resources inevitably triumph over those with less access.

The problem with the socialist societies we have seen around the world, whether we call them communist or socialist, is that they were not democratic enough. Socialism is a system that benefits the majority; therefore, it has to be more, not less, democratic than capitalism. What happened in what we call the communist societies is that a bureaucracy developed that ruled in its own interest. With no electoral democracy, this bureaucracy became much less accountable than capitalist governments in the West. In revolutionary Russia, for example, state terror that was at first used to suppress the counter-revolution was then expanded and used to maintain the power and privilege of the new leaders. They excluded from participation in the affairs of state the very people whom the revolutionaries who fought to transform society were fighting for.

It is tragic to me that capitalism is twinned with democracy in the public mind and socialism with authoritarianism. Patriarchal political parties have produced top-down versions of socialism that exclude the very people who should have been shaping the policies of a socialist regime. Bureaucracies develop that are more interested in self-preservation than in the public interest. While early socialists understood the limitations of electoral democracy, they failed to see that it is also an essential building block of a democratic state. Political rights, such as the rights to vote, free speech, freedom of assembly, and freedom of religion and political belief, are necessary for democracy, although they are not sufficient. Without them, there is no check on absolute power. In the 1960s, those of us who saw the limitations of representative democracy hoped that societies based on collective principles would eventually develop individual rights, but history has proven us wrong. Whatever the good intentions of revolutionary leaders, only strong and unassailable civil and political rights can ensure a democratic society.

Unfortunately, even those social-democratic parties that rejected the authoritarian notions of communism never really understood the importance of the democratic involvement of ordinary people to the capacity to achieve socialism. Social democrats have become enamoured of parliamentary paternalism, often rejecting direct democracy in favour of the most overblown claims for representative democracy. Meanwhile, those of us who first formed our ideas in the New Left successfully brought the politics of social equality and environmentalism into the liberal, social-democratic, and communist movements, but we left the ideas of participatory democracy at the door. Elitism is very seductive when you are invited to become part of the elite.

If the idea that society's wealth can be more fairly distributed is to remain significant, it must be paired with the idea that all people in society will have a say in how the decisions that affect their lives are made. Karl Marx's idea was that only the nationalization of the means of production can lead us to a more democratic and egalitarian society. I believe instead that widening the scope of democracy will lead us to a more socialist society. By placing more and more power in the hands of people who have nothing to gain by maintaining the status quo, we will move down the road towards social and economic equality. But you don't have to be a socialist to accept the ideas of participatory democracy.

The idea that citizens can truly participate in the development and implementation of government policy that affects them is not being promoted by anyone in the political arena in Canada. Yet the public is very interested in it. A 1998 Ekos Research Associates survey called *Rethinking Citizen Engagement,* prepared for a conference of the same name, found strong support for more direct public participation in the decision-making process. Seventy-seven percent of the 2,000 Canadians asked said that today's citizens were better educated and informed and should have more say in decisions. Sixty-eight percent said that big national problems could be solved at the grass-roots level. Fifty-two percent disagreed with the assertion that citizens didn't have the time or the knowledge to offer useful advice on complex issues. Seventy-eight percent said they believed average citizens should have more influence in the political process, and only 26 percent thought that they already did.

But instead of democratizing the state, the right wants to restrict its activities. Progressive groups, including social-reform organizations, feel so under siege by the right wing's attacks on the welfare state that they can respond only by defending it against cutbacks and privatization. A true progressive critique of the state will have to wait until the right-wing assault is turned back. In the meantime, the right-wing critique of the state as inefficient and wasteful rings true with much of the public. The arrogance of the welfare state is obvious to any citizen who comes in contact with government services or to any worker in a government department. Nevertheless, the solution is not to privatize the welfare state, but to democratize it.

Our civil service is still based on a hierarchical military model of command. High-level civil servants develop policy options for their ministers and implement them once decisions are made, but they have little or no contact with the people whom these policies affect. Public consultation is viewed as an ordeal to be suffered rather than an opportunity to unearth new ideas and solutions to difficult problems. Cutbacks have made the situation much worse for front-line government workers who want to better serve their clients.

Meanwhile, right-wing governments like Mike Harris's in Ontario have dispensed with the ritual of consultation altogether. In fact, Harris is getting rid of much of the democratic infrastructure that has been developed over the past thirty years. School boards, one of the most successful examples of local democracy, have been gutted. City governments have been amalgamated so that they are less capable of getting real input from their citizens. Stakeholders who are critical of the government are excluded from the decision-making process altogether.

In the absence of an alternative vision from the left, the neo-liberal approach has now captured the entire political spectrum. I think we have to turn neo-liberalism on its head, as Lula da Silva has tried to do. If neo-liberalism represents the interests of the elite of society, then a new progressive agenda has to represent the interests of the majority of the people. The first item on that agenda must be to engage citizens in political change, in participating in the decisions that affect their lives. As a socialist, I believe that true participatory democracy will result in collective solutions to society's problems.

Democracy is the most powerful tool for social change history has ever seen. We must set out some proposals for how we can move in the direction of truly democratizing our society. We must learn how to take the best from our current form of government and combine it with ideas about direct and participatory democracy that have been developing around the world. Let's call the result active citizenship.

3

GLOBALIZATION'S ASSAULT
ON DEMOCRACY

IN 1969, LIKE MANY YOUNG PEOPLE at the time, I set off on an adventure with no plans. I landed in London and went wherever the spirit and the transportation moved me. I didn't know much about feminism, but what I did know was that I would do just about anything people said I, as a woman, wasn't supposed to do. I travelled alone through Europe, which I found no worse than I had found living alone in New York the year before. There were hassles, but none I couldn't handle. Then I travelled over land to India, which turned out to be exceedingly dangerous and overwhelmingly scary, but that's another story.

When I was stuck in Delhi with a fever that felt like it would be my last, my parents called and offered to pay my way home via Japan to Vancouver, where my brother then lived. On my way, I decided that I wanted to go to China more than anything in the world. The cultural revolution was coming to a close and China was beginning to open its doors. At that point in time, only French citizens were being allowed in, but with the optimism of youth, I thought my left-wing politics would make me an exception. After a five-hour interview at the China News Agency in Hong Kong,

I was told to wait two weeks for an answer. I couldn't afford to wait two weeks in Hong Kong for a pipe dream, so my trip to China was delayed two decades, to the period when the country began to open up to the West. I finally made my trip in November 1987, when my old friend Susan Colley and I decided to go on a four-week vacation.

In 1987, China felt like a pre-revolutionary society. Everyone who lived there wanted to talk to us about democracy. A few were interested in capitalism too, but most of the people I met were excited about gaining more democratic rights. In Shanghai, there was actually a square called Democracy Park, a place where people went to debate and discuss in English and Chinese. I heard a very sophisticated debate there about whether the most important changes happening in China were political or economic. Most people agreed that democratic rights were much more important than what they called the new economy, or capitalism. The tanks at Tiananmen Square in 1989 changed all that.

I went to China again in 1995 to attend the UN NGO Conference on Women. The first sign of the dramatic changes that had taken place in China since my last trip were the billboards on the way out of the airport. There were ads for Canon, Hewlett-Packard, and even the Beijing Golf and Country Club. In 1987, the only posters had been government propaganda posters. Corporate globalization had spread through China like a virus since my last visit, but the new emphasis on a market economy was not bringing about democracy.

As the conference was not to start until the next evening, a group of us decided to go sightseeing. First stop: Tiananmen Square. Winnie Ng, who had been a leader of the pro-democracy solidarity movement in Canada, wore black. She and I entered the square together. I was overwhelmed with a sense of terrible sadness. We both wept quietly for the tremendous potential that had been lost in that struggle. The monument of the People's Heroes, which was where most of the speeches took place during the pro-democracy demonstrations, was cordoned off. I was struck with a powerful desire to place flowers on the monument, to do something to honour the protesters.

A single man facing down the tanks in Tiananmen Square is one of our most enduring images of the struggle for democracy. That particular struggle was crushed, but none of us doubts that some day the Chinese people will win the democratic rights that young man was fighting for. What is in doubt is what these rights mean at the turn of the century. What do democratic rights mean in a world where a small elite is imposing its will through instruments of economic domination and cultural assimilation instead of instruments of mass destruction?

In his book *When Corporations Rule the World,* anti-corporate activist David C. Korten reports that from 1980, which was the beginning of the World Bank–IMF structural adjustment programs, to 1992, the disparity of imports over exports in low-income nations increased from $6.5 billion to $34.7 billion. In that same period, the international indebtedness of those countries increased from $134 billion to $473 billion. According to the Jubilee 2000 Coalition, which is seeking to eliminate debt for the globe's poorest countries by the year 2000, each person in the Third World now owes about $500 to the West, a sum that is much more than a year's wage for many. Africa spends four times as much money on debt repayment as it does on health care.

What happens in these countries is that more and more money is earmarked for interest payments, and government spending on services for citizens decreases. Governments borrow money to pay their debts, racking up even higher debts in the process, and then have to borrow more money to pay the new debts. Instead of spending money on improving the lives of their own citizens, borrowing countries are paying back the banks and other investors.

According to Korten, in Latin America the portion of government spending allocated to interest payments increased from 9 percent to 19.3 percent between 1980 and 1987. In Africa, it rose from 7.7 percent to 12.5 percent. "In their roles as international debt collectors, the World Bank and the IMF have become increasingly intrusive in dictating the public policies of indebted countries and undermining progress toward democratic governance and public accountability," writes Korten. In other words, international bureaucrats are imposing public policy on a host of Third World countries. This policy, called structural adjustment, establishes the kind of economic system we are beginning to become used to in Canada. Cuts in social services, particularly for the poor, privatization, deregulation, and fiscal restraint have an even more devastating impact in poor countries than they have in our own. According to Jonathan Cahn, writing in the *Harvard Human Rights Journal*, "[World] Bank–approved consultants often rewrite a country's trade policy, fiscal policies, civil service requirements, labour laws, health care arrangements, environmental regulations, energy policy, resettlement requirements, procurement rules and budgetary policies." He who pays the piper, in other words, calls the tune.

The famed civil-rights activist and American presidential candidate Jesse Jackson has been quoted as saying, "They [the oppressors] no longer use bullets and ropes. They use the World Bank and the IMF." There is no element of democracy here. According to Korten, "The internal operating processes of the World Bank are so secretive that access to many of its most important documents relating to country plans, strategies and priorities is denied to even its own government directors."

Deepening democracy in the South becomes more and more difficult because of the "solutions" imposed by the World Bank and the IMF, not to mention the even harsher discipline of international investors, who can collapse an economy in an instant if they decide to withdraw their money. The combination of these intrusive monetary policies and the effusive expansion of global consumerism has massively changed the political culture.

In 1965, the political theorist C. B. Macpherson developed his thoughts on the nature of democracy for CBC Radio's Massey lectures. Reading those lectures now illustrates how dramatically the world has changed in the final decades of the twentieth century. In one, he wrote:

It has to be said at once that the underdeveloped countries have on the whole rejected the most characteristic features of liberal-democracy. . . . The competitive market society, which is the soil in which liberal ideas and the liberal state flourish, was not natural to them. Insofar as they knew the market society, it was something imposed on them from outside and from above. Their traditional culture was generally not attuned to competition. They generally saw no intrinsic value in wealth-getting and gave no respect to motive of individual gain. Equality and community, equality within a community, were traditionally rated more highly than individual freedom.

Macpherson suggested that we could expand our own ideas of democracy by learning from various societies in the developing world. Instead, we have brutally imposed our ideas about economics and how society should work upon them. India's Dr. Vandana Shiva, a physicist and environmentalist, calls it the imposition of a monoculture throughout the world. Diversity is crushed rather than cherished.

In an article in *Le Monde diplomatique* in the summer of 1997, Sub-Commandante Marcos of the Zapatista National Liberation Army in Mexico called globalization the Fourth World War (the third was the Cold War). "All the cultures forged by nations — the noble past of American First Nations, the brilliant civilizations of Europe, the wise history of the Asian nations and the rich ancestry of Africa and Oceania — are being eaten away by the American way," he wrote. "Neo-liberalism thus imposes the destruction of nations and groups of nations for the foundation of a single model. Neo-liberalism wages a planetary war, the worst and most cruel, against humanity."

From slavery to colonialism, exploitation has always been part of human society. But corporate globalization reaches even further into the lives of people around the globe than colonialism or imperialism ever did. Resistance seems futile. Economic policies that are deliberately designed to enrich a minority at the expense of the majority are made to appear to be the only alternative. When tanks and torturers crush democratic expression, organizing resistance may be dangerous, but as history has shown, those struggling for freedom cannot be stopped forever by repression. When the instrument of repression is the slow erosion of democracy through the imposition of a single economic system, however, it is much more difficult to dream of the day when this repression will be overturned. But it is the dream, whether of freedom, democracy, or equality, that motivates people to organize resistance on a mass scale. Convincing people that there is no alternative to inequity is the most insidious form of repression. Persuading people that no collective solutions are possible and that a better world lies in informed self-interest is the slyest means yet invented of eroding democratic participation.

Corporate globalization forces countries in the Third World to reorganize in a neo-liberal direction and puts pressure on governments to carry out those policies that are most likely to translate into corporate profit. You know the list: free trade, cutbacks, privatization, deregulation, balanced budget, tax cuts, smaller public sector. The market knows best. The private sector is more efficient than the public sector. Services can be delivered more effectively by private interests. Some neo-liberal ideologues go so far as to say that individuals have more power as consumers than they do as citizens. After all, the story goes, governments don't respond to citizens, but the marketplace does respond to consumers; thus consumer power is more potent than people's power.

The impact of international capital, trade agreements, and the Bretton Woods institutions on national governments has turned the attention of many activists to the global situation. On one level, this is a correct response to corporate globalization, for sometimes the unimaginable can happen when groups band together. The defeat — or at least derailment — of the Multilateral Agreement on Investment (MAI), for example, was the result of an international lobby campaign led in part by our own Council of Canadians.

The MAI was, as the activist Tony Clarke put it, NAFTA on steroids. Its imposition would have even more severely restricted our governments' ability to make policy that meets the needs of citizens. The most disturbing provision of the MAI was the right given to corporations to sue a national government if they felt that a law or regulation was interfering with their ability to make a profit. This provision already exists in watered-down form in NAFTA. And if you think corporations couldn't get away with that here, look what happened when the Canadian government tried to ban the neurotoxin MMT from use in gasoline: the Ethyl Corporation sued for restraint of trade, and the government, rather than fight a costly lawsuit, paid a $19-million out-of-court settlement, dropped the ban, and issued a statement saying there was no evidence that MMT was dangerous. Where is democracy if government initiatives can be overturned not in the public interest but in the profit interests of a single multinational corporation?

Even without the MAI, the World Trade Organization (WTO) is forcing drastic changes to Canadian policy based on trade complaints from other countries. At the time of this writing, the WTO had just ruled against the Auto Pact, which has been the driving force of the Ontario economy since 1965. The Auto Pact provides tariff protection for the big four American auto manufacturers in return for their commitment to produce one vehicle in Canada for every vehicle sold here, thus guaranteeing Canadian jobs. Japan and the European Community have argued that the pact is an unfair trade practice, and the WTO agreed. Even more disturbing is the expected victory of the United States and the European Union in striking down our drug-patent legislation. Most health activists believe that the federal government has already given away the store to patent drug manufacturers, but the WTO wants the legislation tilted even more in their favour. The results for Canadians: even more expensive prescription drugs and higher costs for provinces that have drug programs.

Where the market rules, money rules and public interest is not even a factor. As the economist Adam Smith once put it, "The vile

51

maxim of capitalists is everything for ourselves and nothing for anyone else." Mainstream economists convince us that self-interest is the only rational motivating force, and that society has to be the craziest concept that ever motivated civilization. These ideas, which have come to dominate the world economy, do work well for a small minority of the rich and powerful. For most of us, however, they mean ever-declining standards of living and more and more insecurity. C. B. Macpherson said, in his 1965 Massey lectures:

> I want to suggest that our moral and political theory took the wrong turning when it began to interpret the human essence as possession or acquisition.
>
> Men [*sic*] are not by nature infinitely desirous creatures, but were only made so by the market society, which compelled men to seek even greater power in order to maintain even a modest level of satisfaction.
>
> Individuals and nations in the liberal democratic world, after centuries of operating their competitive market societies, are so accustomed to acquisitive behaviour and seeking power over others that they cannot easily be got out of this frame of mind. It may be economically possible now for them to drop it; it may be desirable that they should drop it; but how can they drop it when the whole structure of their society has come to depend on power-seeking, both individual and national, both economic and political?

Instead of dropping acquisition and power over others, corporate globalization has reinforced it beyond where Macpherson feared it would go. The majority of people are getting poorer and even less powerful. The trade-union movement, the most important counterpoint to corporate power in the twentieth century, has been significantly weakened in most developed countries. Social movements that originated in the 1960s have been either co-opted or marginalized. Political parties that once delineated clear differences between left and right, each representing specific class interests, are looking more and more like one another. Instead of articulating a different vision of society — one where working people, rather than the capitalist elite, exercise control from the bottom up — social-democratic parties have been reduced to making capitalism a little more humane — but not enough to interfere with raging profit, of course.

If it is true that multinational corporations have inordinate power and influence in our society today, it is equally true that national governments have allowed them to grow unchecked; they are becoming bigger and more powerful by ingesting everything in their path. The environmentalist David Suzuki tells us that cancer is the only organism in nature that grows without limit. The cancer of multinational corporations has been allowed to spread across the globe with barely any attempt to contain it.

Lula da Silva, whom we met in the previous chapter, told me that wherever the Workers Party has power in Brazil, neo-liberalism is turned on its head. Instead of basing decisions on what is in the best interests of multinational corporations and investors, the members of the Workers Party base them on the best interests of the poor and disenfranchised. They do this not through a benevolent, patronizing state, but by giving citizens the tools and the structures to participate in the decision-making process.

Turning the neo-liberal model upside down may be a useful way to come up with alternatives. If neo-liberalism thrives on secretive, hierarchical organizations that use financial power to impose uniform solutions on every country, then a more economically just society should thrive on local and regional democratic organizations that develop priorities based on the needs of people within their own communities. There is no turning back from globalization, but we can introduce global relationships based on a valuing of diversity, a respect for the democratic decisions of individual countries, and a privileging of equality over dominance.

The UN NGO women's conference in China discussed what globalization based on equality might look like. Just the experience itself gave me a glimpse of what people's globalization could mean. On the first day of the conference, I had the extraordinary feeling of being in a multicultural city of women. Here it was the sensibility of women that prevailed. African women were dressed in spectacular costume, and all the rest of us looked pallid in comparison. And most extraordinarily, the big women looked better in these outfits than the thin ones. Suddenly beauty was redefined. This was a woman-centred universe marred only by the occasional intrusion of apparently irrational Chinese bureaucracy.

At the opening ceremonies, I was overwhelmed by the reality of being in a sports stadium filled with women. The most male of all public facilities had been transformed. I seemed to be in the Arab section of the stadium. In front of me were rows of Tunisian women in Western dress but with Tunisian flags. They broke out into a desert chant at the slightest prompting. To my left was a group of Kuwaiti women, most of whom were in chadors or veils, and all of whom wore matching baseball caps. A veiled woman in a baseball cap, cheering in unison with her sisters at every mention of women's equality, is surely one of the most contradictory images I have ever seen. But my assumptions and biases were challenged throughout the course of that extraordinary adventure.

As they filed out of the stadium, women gathered in groups to sing and to dance. Outside the stadium, two African women were selling cloth and bags made out of the same material as the dresses they were wearing. Female entrepreneurship was to be another constant feature of the conference.

In the 1960s, we called it internationalism. The idea was that people around the world could work together for mutual benefit without exploitation. Of course, back then a lot of our notions of internationalism were pretty romantic and idealistic, and were based on the desire of youth rather than the reality of capitalism. That idealism, nevertheless, is a good framework for developing a vision of what a people's globalization, rather than the corporate globalization we have now, could look like.

The need to democratize international institutions like the World Bank and the IMF was a major preoccupation at the Beijing Women's Conference. During the first of the conference's twice-daily plenary sessions, Gita Sen, representing Development Alternatives for Women in a New Era (DAWN), talked about the rapidity of globalization and its capacity to undermine the economic role of the state and its ability to provide services. She said the Bretton Woods institutions have acted like storm troopers, breaking the resistance of the state. What has not been undermined, she adds, are the repressive forces of the state. "Governments that can no longer provide even minimal health and education are [still] maintaining huge arsenals."

Sen also described a resurgence of patriarchal forces in the guise of fundamentalism, ethnic chauvinism, and religious orthodoxy. Then, just as it all began to seem too overwhelming, she added that the women's movement can take advantage of globalization. She identified what are for her the three crucial parts of any struggle for equality and justice: challenging the negative economic forces unleashed by globalization; transforming international institutions and states to make them more accountable; and creating the institutions of a civil society.

Winnie Karagwa Byanyima from Uganda reinforced the message. There is something wrong, she argued, when Africa, the poorest continent, spends $8 billion a year on armaments. She said that globalization has fractured the continent's family and spiritual values, and that only the fundamentalists are responding to the need for spiritual renewal. She proposed that we struggle for a system of governance based on equality, that we restructure global financial institutions to reflect these values, and that we strive for a global culture that is multicultural, not monocultural.

Charlotte Bunch, from the U.S., concluded the opening plenary session by saying that we are being given a choice: accept globalization and all that it represents or accept a return to traditional patriarchal values. She argued that the women's movement had to struggle for a third option.

I was struck by the commonality of the analyses presented by women from three continents. Thanks to all the participants, the extraordinarily complex impact of globalization was revealed over the course of the conference. It is hard to imagine such a conference — with women from around the world sharing common ideas and, in some ways, a common woman-positive culture — taking place in any other era. The experiences of Third World women with the structural adjustment policies of the World Bank and the IMF prefigure the experiences we are now having in the North with debt and deficit mania and the accompanying onslaught against our social programs and economic rights.

But the most powerful and warmly received speech didn't strike the same reform-minded note that the others had. In fact, Winona LaDuke, co-chair of the Indigenous Women's Network and a member of the Mississippi band of the Anishinabe people, completely rejected all notions of restructuring corporate capitalism. It was the most radical speech I've heard in twenty years. LaDuke's focus was on the rights of indigenous people and on the destruction of the environment. She asked what law had given away the land of her people to corporations.

> Decision making is not done by those who are affected by the decisions, people who live on the land, but [by] corporations with an interest which is entirely different [from] that of the land and [of] the people, or the women of the land. This brings forth a fundamental question: What gives these corporations, like Conoco, Shell, Exxon, . . . and the World Bank, a right which supersedes or is superior to my human right to live on the land, or [is superior to] that of my family, my community, my nation, our nations, and to us as women? What law gives that right to them?. . . Is that right contained within their wealth? Is that right contained within their wealth that is his-

torically acquired immorally, unethically, through colonialism, imperialism, and paid for with the lives of millions of people, or species of plants and entire ecosystems? They should have no such right. . . .

The origins of this problem lie with the predator/prey relationship [that] industrial society has developed with the Earth and, subsequently, the people of the Earth. This same relationship exists vis-à-vis women. We, collectively, find that we are often in the role of the prey to a predator society, whether for sexual discrimination, exploitation, sterilization, absence of control over our bodies, or being the subjects of repressive laws and legislation in which we have no voice. This occurs on an individual level, but equally, and more significantly, on a societal level.

LaDuke further asserted that the North-South analysis was not correct for aboriginal people. "It is the temperate middle that is consuming both the North and the South," she argued. "Women should not have to trade their ecosystems for running water. . . . With industrial development, women are moved from the centre of our societies to the margins."

LaDuke's conclusion was that in a society dominated by the interests of a few multinational corporations and international investment companies, only radical and fundamental change was possible. Surprisingly, she received a standing ovation. An Associated Press reporter sitting next to me said, "I'll bet they didn't know what they were getting into when they invited her." Somehow, I think they did.

LaDuke represents the point of view of a growing number of international activists who see the overthrow of corporate rule as the only possible route to social change. Naomi Klein is a progressive young journalist who researched the anti-corporate youth movement for her book *No Logo,* which was published early in the year 2000. "There is this free-flowing rage against multinational corporations among young people," says Klein. "It's a backlash that was waiting to happen." The Battle of Seattle protests against the WTO at the end of 1999 have been the most visible and dramatic expression of that rage.

Klein argues that the anti-corporate movement that is now sweeping across campuses in the United States and through the streets of England was caused by the collision of three major forces. The first force is the loss of public space epitomized by ads in schools and ads in bathrooms. Companies have aggressively infiltrated every aspect of public space. The second is protection lost because there is less and less connection between a particular company and jobs in the community. And the third is that corporations are much more visible. Millions and millions are spent to promote their logos and burn their names into our consciousness.

The aggressive corporate campaign to infiltrate every corner of public space has produced an international grass-roots resistance movement. According to Klein, multinational corporations have become the target of movements like this because of their obvious power and, most important, because of the loss of connection between jobs and profit. "Nike is the symbol of this corporate disconnect because they have totally severed marketing from any sense that you might get a job from them," she told me in an interview. "Nowhere is this more pronounced than in the inner city. They are feeding off the culture of black youth in the inner city without providing jobs. They've made themselves into tribal icons, but they've also lost their protection." When she is asked where this resistance to corporate rule is headed, Klein responds: "The most lasting legacy of the 1960s is this unwillingness to actually commit to where this movement is going. At this point, it is enough to have a critique and resist, and that's about as far as it goes. Which isn't to say that it's not radical."

These youth movements are growing and feeding each other over the Internet. Indeed, worldwide movements for social change have never been more possible. Young activists who were trying to unionize McDonald's in Quebec, for example, linked up with the British reformers who were behind the famous McLibel suit; soon the two groups were sharing strategies and information through e-mail. On June 18, 1999, the Reclaim the Streets movement organized a global day of resistance to capitalism that saw as many as 10,000 young people out on the streets in Britain and Australia. International solidarity among women's groups through the United Nations has created momentum around issues like violence against women that might never have happened in just one country. The Fédération des Femmes du Québec, for example, is sponsoring a global women's march against poverty and violence that will take place in almost 200 countries around the world between March and October 2000. Thousands of protestors turned Seattle upside down in December 1999, focusing the attention of the world on the powerful anti-democratic WTO. These kinds of initiatives have been made possible by the advent of the Internet and e-mail.

Women's, aboriginal, and anti-poverty groups have effectively used the United Nations to embarrass the Canadian government about its record on human-rights issues. In fact, this may have been the key effort in the campaign to earn aboriginal women the right to retain their status if they marry a non-aboriginal man. When poor people in Canada were faced with continued cuts to social assistance, they turned to the UN committee that monitors the International Covenant on Economic, Social and Cultural Rights and asked it to hold the country accountable. The committee issued a devastating report that denounced Canada for fighting the deficit on the backs of the poor. That report helped to open up some public space for the debate about poverty and homelessness.

Many groups are trying to use the United Nations as a democratic alternative to corporate globalization. Canadian anti-poverty activists, for example, are turning to the United Nations for help implementing the idea of a rights-based approach to ending poverty. The UN International Covenant on Economic, Social and Cultural Rights, which Canada has signed, ensures the right of everyone to food and shelter. Anti-poverty groups have been fighting to have that right, along with the right to be free from discrimination based on social status, enshrined by the courts in our Charter of Rights and Freedoms.

Activists want to turn the UN covenants into enforceable law with as much clout as the directives of the IMF, the World Bank, and the WTO. Unfortunately, the UN, which was founded at the same time as these Bretton Woods institutions and is much more democratic, has much less power. Nevertheless, activists have made some dramatic gains through the United Nations, particularly in the areas of women's and environmental issues.

Yet it is hard to imagine democratizing global institutions without democratizing national, provincial, and local ones as well. While grass-roots movements can certainly develop and grow globally through electronic organizing, the role of the nation-state kicks in as soon as any significant attempt is made to influence the international institutions we've discussed in this chapter. However undemocratic these various international institutions may be, they all rely on nation-states for their ultimate power. So in the end, it is the struggle at home that makes the difference.

4

THE FEMINIZATION OF POLITICS

FROM AMONG THE RATHER EXCESSIVELY flattering speeches made about me the night I stepped down as president of NAC on June 6, 1993, I remember one comment most clearly. "When I think of Judy," said Carolann Wright, a black community activist from Halifax who was then living in Toronto, "I think of big ears." We all laughed, because of course most people would think of a big mouth first. But Wright explained that what she valued most about me was that I listened. I learned a lot about leadership from that one remark.

For me, learning to listen was the hardest leadership skill to master. As a woman in a man's world, I had always believed my most important communication skill was my ability to talk. Whether I was fighting with my father, standing up for myself in a male-dominated left-wing organization, or vying for media attention as a pro-choice advocate, I needed to make my voice heard. But when I began working with people with even less access to power or space, I soon realized that it was more important to listen.

From 1975 to 1990, with a couple of breaks, I worked for the Canadian Hearing Society. Working with deaf and hard-of-hearing people and others with various disabilities taught me my first lesson in how to listen without imposing my own world-view. Then a few years in therapy showed me a model of listening that I had never seen before. A good therapist trains for years to learn how to listen to what her patient is saying without passing immediate judgement. Politicians learn to do the opposite. They listen only to find an opening to tell you what they think. As Arlene Perly Rae once said about her husband, former NDP Ontario premier Bob Rae, "Bob's idea of listening is waiting before speaking again."

When I became president of NAC, my gift of the gab was a bonus outside the organization. But inside, it was an obstacle. I discovered, in mediating a couple of internal disputes, that what people say and what other people hear are not necessarily the same thing. It was only by temporarily putting aside my own views and just listening to what the other person was saying without arguing back — at least right away — that I could actually understand the point being made. So that is what I tried to do with the women of colour, lesbians, women with disabilities, and poor women I met in NAC.

I don't believe that a white woman cannot represent the interests of women of colour or that a man cannot represent the interests of women. Human solidarity is an essential element of any society. If we cannot empathize with others in different circumstances, what hope do we have of building a more democratic, more equitable society? But our own society is so hierarchically structured that the reality lived by, let's say, white middle-class women in urban centres is very different from that of poor black women in the same city. As the gap between rich and poor grows, the gap in shared lived experience becomes even greater. The fewer universal public services, the greater the gap once again. In a society such as ours, we have to work very hard to hear what a person from a different gender, race, class, or sexual orientation is saying.

Remember the debate surrounding Robert Latimer's killing of his severely disabled daughter Tracy in 1993? When people with disabilities first spoke out about their fears of genocide if Latimer's actions were justified by a court, my non-disabled friends and most of the media were either horrified or thought it was an overreaction. Most able-bodied people immediately identified with Latimer, the father who couldn't bear to see his terribly disabled daughter suffer another day. People with disabilities, meanwhile, identified with Tracy, the daughter who couldn't even tell her father what her life, even with the terrible pain, meant to her.

Beryl Potter and Sam Savona taught me how it is impossible to judge people who live a different reality without hearing from them about their own experiences. Potter was the most enthusiastic, active advocate I've ever known, despite being a triple amputee who was in constant pain. The group we co-chaired, Disabled People for Employment Equity, organized a 1988 demonstration in Ottawa to protest the passage of the new Employment Equity Act, which we thought was not strong enough. After the demo, we piled into the visitors gallery in the House of Commons. The few accessible seats were rapidly taken up, and since the Speaker would not allow people in wheelchairs on the floor of the Commons, Potter was left outside in the corridor. "Carry me in," she ordered one of the guards. "But, Beryl, can you sit in a regular seat?" I asked, with visions of her falling out of the gallery chair the moment she was placed in it. "I don't know," she answered, "but I'm not missing this debate for the world." Needless to say, the guard miraculously found space for her wheelchair. Potter was a tactical genius.

Sam Savona is the most severely disabled person I know. He cannot feed himself, walk, talk so he is understood by most people, or sit upright unassisted. He is also the most joyful person I've ever met. Not only has he been a constant activist for disabled rights, but he has also run for political office. When I first met both Savona and Potter, my first thought was, How can they live like that? I didn't think I could ever do it. But over the years, they transformed my understanding of disability. As a result, I was one of the few non-religious, non-disabled people in the country who thought Latimer should have been convicted of murder.

One of Karl Marx's most brilliant observations was that being determines consciousness. The circumstances of your life have an enormous impact on how you see the world around you. The most dramatic evidence we have of Marx's observation is the extraordinary gender gap in politics that has emerged with the influence of feminism.

Gender is as decisive a cleavage as region, age, or income. Yet until recently, political parties in Canada have paid scant attention to it. In all the discussion surrounding the tenth anniversary of the Free Trade Agreement (FTA), for example, no one mentioned the enormous gender gap that characterized Canadians' opinions in 1988. Elisabeth Gidengil, a political scientist at McGill University, found a sixteen-point gender gap in 1988 polls, with women opposing the FTA and men supporting it. This translated to an eight-point gender gap in party preference, with men supporting Brian Mulroney's Tories more than women. When Gidengil examined the reasons for the gap, she found that for women free trade seemed to be a social issue, while for men it was more of an economic issue. No doubt the high-profile presence on the anti–free trade side of NAC's vice-president, Marjorie Cohen, and the Council of Canadians' Maude Barlow also influenced women. After the 1988 election, many English Canadians who opposed free trade were bitter about Quebec's strong support of the Tories, which gave Mulroney his majority. Perhaps they should have blamed men instead.

The gender gap also helped determine the outcome of another crucial vote: the Quebec sovereignty referendum of 1995. In a CROP poll, only 41 percent of female respondents in the province said they would vote Yes in the referendum, compared with 49 percent of males. Again, women's greatest concern was the impact of sovereignty on social programs. Instead of money and the ethnic vote, perhaps Jacques Parizeau should have blamed women.

In an interview in 1998, Donna Dasko, vice-president of Environics Research Group, told me, "I am almost never asked about the gender gap. Nobody cares about it." Then, to my astonishment, she said the women's vote gave the Liberals their majority in the 1997 federal election. "If only men had voted," Dasko explained, "there would have been a minority Liberal government." Think of all the headlines in that election that were devoted to regional difference: Reform in the West, the Liberals in Ontario, the Bloc Québécois in Quebec, Tories and the NDP in Atlantic Canada. Do you remember reading anything about the Liberals owing their majority to women? During the campaign, only one reporter asked Dasko about the gender gap. She had to — she was writing a story about how little impact women were having in the election.

The gender gap in Canada was first recognized in the early 1980s, although as early as 1974 support for Pierre Trudeau was six points higher among women than men. In 1984 in the United States, Ronald Reagan's right-wing platform and the presence of Geraldine Ferraro as the Democratic vice-presidential candidate combined to produce a significant gender gap. In Canada, meanwhile, all three federal parties agreed to a NAC-sponsored women's debate. The results have become political legend. Both Brian Mulroney and John Turner saw their support among women decline after the debate, even though each had promised a deep commitment to women's equality. Of course, women could see they were lying through their teeth. After that momentary brush with valuing women's political concerns, both the Liberals and the Tories quickly returned with relief to the comfortable male world.

In the United States, where gender is one of the few fundamental divides between the two mainstream parties, a lot of fairly superficial analysis has given us the idea that women support the Democrats because they are more compassionate and men the Republicans because they are more concerned with money and the status quo. But on closer examination, the gender gap turns out to be not so easy to explain or understand.

Surprisingly, there is no significant gender gap on what we traditionally view as women's issues. Abortion, childcare, and even pay and employment equity are issues that are supported equally by men and women. But this seems to belie the "angry white male" explanation heard so often in the United States during the 1994 Contract with America election, which saw the Newt Gingrich Republicans win majorities in both the House and the Senate. Steven Stark based his analysis of the election in a 1996 *Atlantic Monthly* article on the "angry white male" model. "The new Republican Party [was] built around the opposition of white southern males to the sexual and race revolutions," he wrote, noting that when Alabama's governor George Wallace ran for president as a backlash candidate in 1968, two-thirds of his supporters were male. Another American writer, Todd Gitlin, wrote, in his book *The Twilight of Common Dreams*, "Many men demonized as conservative white males will ironically seek out the very stereotypical identity with which they have been tagged."

In Canada, the Reform Party, like other right-wing parties, experiences a dramatic gender gap: more than twice as many men as women support it. In British Columbia, evidence suggests that a significant number of federal Reform supporters vote NDP provincially. No one has examined whether this shift takes place primarily among males. I asked Bill Tieleman, a former B.C. NDP strategist, if he thought any of this move to Reform was a backlash against women's equality. "The main reason," he told me, "was that after Charlottetown and Meech, the NDP started to look like part of the establishment. Reform looked like the anti-establishment party." Interestingly, Tieleman had no idea whether most of the people who had moved over to Reform were men. He had never looked at the gender divide. Reform has its core support among people who might fit the "angry white male" profile developed by U.S. analysts, as does the Conservative Party in Ontario.

More significant than the "angry white male" phenomenon is the impact of the women's movement on the role of women. Since the early 1970s, women have flooded into post-secondary education and into the workforce. During this same period, marital instability increased dramatically. Not surprisingly, single and divorced women diverge politically from men more than married women do. The direct political influence of feminism seems to affect both sexes, but feminism does help create a gender gap by giving women, including married women, the autonomy to think differently from men. As Stark points out in his analysis of the American political scene, "The more men and women were accorded equal treatment in the culture, the less they resembled each other politically. By 1980, for the first time, more than half of all women worked outside the home, and pollsters found that those who did work were far more likely to vote differently from men than those who did not." In that sense, the gender gap is a triumph of feminism, albeit a partial one. The challenge now is to move from the gender gap to the feminization of politics.

Despite suffering through fifteen years of neo-liberal politics, women continue to strongly support the preservation of Canada's social programs. When pollsters ask respondents to list, in order of importance, priorities for the next government (the question that is used to determine the level of support for fiscal conservatism), the gender gap is dramatic. In 1997, 35 percent of men and only 22 percent of women said that reducing the federal deficit was the top priority. By contrast, 30 percent of women prioritized spending on health and social programs, compared with 17 percent of men. The only priority agreed to by equal numbers of men and women was job creation.

A generally accepted explanation for the gender gap on social issues is that women use social services more than men and also work in the public sector more than men, and so view social programs as more worthy of support. Women and children make up the majority of the poor, and women live longer than men and so are more dependent on public pensions. For all these reasons, then, it makes sense that women would support social programs more strongly than men. Yet even when both the influence of feminism and the disparity in income levels are taken out of the equation, as social scientists can do through regression analysis, the gender gap remains on key issues.

To fully understand the gender gap, Elisabeth Gidengil believes that we have to look at the basic differences between men and women as explained by the feminist writer Carol Gilligan. Without taking a position on nature versus nurture, Gilligan says in her famous book *In a Different Voice* that men and women perceive the world in fundamentally different ways. Men are more individual-istic, competitive, and hierarchical, women more collectivist and co-operative. In other words, according to Environics vice-president Jane Armstrong, "Women are more relationship-oriented and more community-oriented."

In a 1995 article in *Foreign Affairs* magazine, the historian Francis Fukuyama writes that one of the reasons democracies are more pacific towards each other than dictatorships is that "developed democracies tend to be more feminized than authoritarian states, in terms of expansion of female franchise and participation in political decision making." He thinks militarism is "bred in the bone" of young men and can't be "tossed off like an old sweater." It seems more likely that it is a side-effect of masculinization.

If the gender gap is a result of immutable differences between women and men, then it should be consistent across countries and cultures, but it is not. In Britain, at least until recently, the gender gap has taken the form of more women supporting the Tories and more men supporting Labour. According to Mary-Ann Stephenson, author of *The Glass Trapdoor: Women, Politics and Media during the 1997 General Election*, "Had women voted the same way as men there would have been a continuous Labour government from 1945 to 1979." In this case, the gender gap had to do with the Tory focus on family and church and Labour's relationship with the mostly male industrial unions. With the rise of right-wing Thatcherism in the 1980s, the gender gap disappeared. In the 1992 election, won by the Tories under John Major, many women returned to the Tory fold, but among younger voters the gender gap was reversed. Fifty-three percent of young men, compared with only 33 percent of young women, voted Tory. By 1997, Tony Blair won even more support from women, thus earning his large majority. Stephenson concludes: "At the 1997 election Labour succeeded in winning the votes of many women for the first time. The scale of Labour's vic-tory in part depended on this historic switch among women voters."

In an interview, the University of Toronto political scientist Sylvia Bashevkin said pro-Tory women tended to be older and "most of them are in the graveyard now. The British gender gap is similar to the North American one." An international study of party support showed that women were more left wing than men in Canada, Germany, Portugal, Spain, Denmark, and the United States. In Britain, Australia, Luxembourg, Italy, Ireland, and France, women were more right wing than men.

But Bashevkin thinks right and left are the wrong filters through which to see the gender gap. "What women support is moderate social reform," Bashevkin explains. "Women don't like extremes of left or right." Other feminist scholars have identified something called gender consciousness, which is produced by a variety of factors, including the influence of the women's movement. Citing the work of the American pollster Celinda Lake, Steven Stark notes that "in a politics defined by gender identification, men are more likely to rally to a male standard than women to a female one. Men still tend to follow conventional politics far more closely than women do: they are more likely to find their identity in it and be energized by it."

In a 1998 Ekos survey titled *Rethinking Citizen Engagement*, 51 percent of men and only 24 percent of women scored high on political literacy. Respondents were rated based on their answers to simple political questions, such as the name of the prime minister and premiers and the number of MPs. Youth under thirty score even lower than women on political literacy. This is important because it indicates exclusion from the political process. Ekos president Frank Graves says, "This index is linked to a range of other indicators, like who is more likely to participate in politics and who is more satisfied with government performance."

So perhaps the gender gap simply reflects the fact that politics is still, by and large, a men's club. And the corporate world, which influences so much of our economic policy, is even more male-dominated. A recent Statistics Canada study shows that only 6 percent of corporate board members are female. Women tend to be much more active in community politics, which in turn reinforces their tendency to value social programs.

The University of Alberta political scientist Janine Brodie says, "What women want [strong social programs] is contrary to the consensus of the elites." When the major political parties decided to support massive cuts to social programs to reduce the deficit, they knew they could no longer count on the women's vote. "Instead," Brodie argues, "they tried to make the gap disappear by removing women as a political category in their language. Women as a policy category disappeared towards the end of Mulroney's last term. By Paul Martin's second budget, women were mentioned only once as a category, and that was [in reference to] nutrition for pregnant women." We no longer speak about the feminization of poverty. Now it's child poverty, even though in most cases children are poor because their parents, and particularly their mothers, are poor. The Speech from the Throne in October 1999 barely mentioned women, even though maternity leave and childcare, two of the highlighted issues, have been top priorities for the women's movement for decades. Now they are both defined as children's issues. It is almost as if "woman" has become as dirty a political word as "feminist."

In this post-deficit era, however, women are becoming a more potent political force. Those political parties that have directly appealed to women have reaped the benefits in the polls and at the ballot box. Ironically, no one has done this more successfully than Bill Clinton, whose high standing in the polls throughout his impeachment troubles was largely a result of his support among women. When Clinton was first elected, the gender gap (in terms of support for Democrats vs. Republicans) was fairly narrow. Today it is up to eleven points — and up to seventeen points between men and women under thirty. The Parti Québécois, meanwhile, has improved its standing among women through its five-dollar-a-day childcare program and its appointment of high-profile women cabinet ministers. In a November 1998 Léger and Léger poll, the PQ had the support of 45 percent of women, the Liberals 44.2 percent. The gender gap had disappeared, although with the PQ's hard-line treatment of striking nurses in the summer of '99, it started to appear again.

Before the 1980s, the NDP/CCF had more support among men than women. Today that gender gap has reversed, not only federally, where the party has had women leaders since 1989, but also at the provincial level. Given how low the NDP's level of popular support has gone, it seems likely that the party can improve its numbers only by appealing to women. Yet recent policy changes, which are moving the party more to the right, would suggest that it is going in the opposite direction. If the NDP listens to the mostly male, mostly neo-liberal media, it will certainly continue on the road to oblivion, gendered or not.

We already know that women's political concerns broadly coincide with a more communitarian approach to politics. Since men who identify with feminism share many of the concerns of women, it should certainly be possible to convince them to place a higher priority on social programs and community values. Indeed, this process has already begun in the trade-union movement, where unions are organizing more and more women without losing their traditional base of support among men. Today, sexist comments or anti-feminist remarks are even more unacceptable in trade-union circles than feminist positions used to be. I occasionally speak at the Paid Education Leave course of the Canadian Auto Workers union, and I am always impressed by the support for women's issues that can be found among rank-and-file auto workers. The first time I saw a big burly guy who looked like a biker get up to the mike to take part in a discussion on violence against women, I braced for the worst, expecting the usual anti-feminist tirade about how women exaggerate the problem. Instead, he spoke from the heart about the beatings his mother had suffered. He even shed a few tears at the mike.

Unions have made enormous progress in empowering their female membership and educating their male membership, but they remain very male-dominated at the leadership level and very patriarchal in their form of organization. Women leaders in the

Canadian Labour Congress (CLC) recently decided to work for feminist organizing models inside the labour movement. If they succeed, it would lead to a deep democratization of the trade-union movement, as well as a broadening of its influence.

The gender gap reveals the links between social issues and the feminization of politics. Any analysis of the gender gap gives new life to the arguments for democratizing and feminizing our organizations and our political parties. The feminization of politics is not only a matter of representation. When a significant number of women are involved, it not only affects the political process, but also changes the policies that come out of that process. For example, it was women inside the Liberal cabinet and caucus who fought for the extension of maternity and parental leave to be high on the government's agenda in the fall of 1999. The popular five-dollar-a-day childcare program in Quebec would never have seen the light of day without the dogged determination of Pauline Marois, the minister of education at the time.

On the other hand, women in mainstream politics have to learn the male game so well that they are often unwilling or unable to challenge the patriarchal processes of politics. Women in mainstream politics too often have to act like men in order to be taken seriously. This was certainly the dynamic for the women who entered Bob Rae's cabinet when the NDP took power in Ontario in 1990. Women who rose to power believing they could change the existing structure through their feminist ideas became Madam Minister faster than you could shake a stick. Even those ministers who at first surrounded themselves with feminist staff soon turned much more towards their male advisers, who were more comfortable operating in the existing power structure. Even though there were enough women ministers to make a difference, they never met together to plan strategies or to challenge the process.

Kim Campbell, who is Canada's only female prime minister to date, has done a lot of thinking about how women politicians are stereotyped. "Women prefer interactive modes of leadership and men prefer command. My gun-control legislation was a good example about how women are judged harshly," she told me in an interview. "I tabled it and sent it to committee before second reading so that MPs could go home to their ridings and have some time to consider the thing before they had to vote on it. I was aware how controversial it was, and I needed time to guide the legislation through. Every time I tacked [to the left or the right], the media said my legislation was being sidelined. I was being an interactive leader making sure I had consulted thoroughly, and the media saw that as weakness. But I never would have gotten the bill through if I had rammed it through.

"There is a profoundly different approach, and it relates to gender," she went on to say. "If official interpreters, the media, don't understand what you are doing, then it won't have an impact. A woman's emphasis on collegiality is seen by men as weakness. Women share power."

I had an experience with Campbell as justice minister where she did share her power, and the political results were completely transformative. In 1991, the Supreme Court struck down the old so-called rape shield law, leaving women open once again to defence attorneys' vicious probing into their sexual history. Campbell responded by proposing a new law that would simply codify the restrictions on when sexual history would be relevant.

But women's groups decided to fight for a better law, one that would define consent. So many accused rapists got off by claiming that they believed they had consent that we felt it was necessary to clearly define the term in the law. Campbell's officials were resistant to the changes, but when we met with the minister herself, she was persuaded. The new "No Means No" law was the result. At the time, you may remember, critics ridiculed the law. They said that couples would need signed consent forms by the bedside, and also that the law would not stand up to constitutional scrutiny. Now it has. The Supreme Court unanimously upheld it, strongly and forcefully, in the spring of 1999.

Of this process, Campbell says, "In theory the bureaucrats in justice could have written the rape shield law, but I knew that we had to include women activists in drafting it for them to support it. I saw with the rape shield law what you can do when you do things differently and include people."

It was the first time that any government had seriously included feminist activists in the process of drafting law. I personally doubt very much that the officials in the justice department could have drafted a law that so well reflected women's experiences, but it is true that our inclusion meant that Campbell had the support of the women, who had been among the harshest critics of her government. This time she got media kudos for bringing women's groups on side.

Feminists often talk about how a critical mass of women is necessary to transform the political process and make it more attuned to the concerns of women. But my experience tells me that unless the political structures are changed, any women we manage to elect will be sucked up into the power elite and begin behaving very much like their male colleagues. Active citizenship will give women in elected and bureaucratic positions of power the support they need to do things differently. If the proper supports are in place, women are also much more likely to participate in grass-roots democracy than in the more formal models of representative democracy. No project for active citizenship is possible without the full participation and leadership of women.

5

Citizen Engagement

At that same meeting with Kim Campbell to discuss the draft legislation for a new rape law, something else miraculous happened. As soon as Campbell had agreed to our proposal and invited the LEAF (the Legal Education and Action Fund) lawyers in our group to work with her officials, Lee Lakeman, a twenty-five-year veteran of the anti-violence movement and the gutsiest woman I've ever met, said, "No, we can't do that. We have to consult directly with the women whose lives will be affected by this law: anti-violence workers, survivors, and the groups most vulnerable to sexual assault — prostitutes, aboriginals, and young women. And we need you [the minister] to pay for us to have that consultation, so it can be truly representative." I couldn't believe it. We had just got concessions beyond our wildest dreams and Lee was asking for more.

But Campbell wanted the bill passed quickly, that Christmas. She didn't want to wait for a more democratic process to take place. Wasn't our group representative enough? she asked. Lakeman hung tough, explaining that we couldn't do to our constituents what the government does to us all the time — that is, assume that we are speaking for them. The drafting of this law would involve major decisions that would deeply affect the lives of thousands of women. We had to make sure to do it right. Yet Lakeman's concern was not at all that our members would be angry with us for participating in the drafting of the bill without their consent. On the contrary, they would simply have been thrilled that we were getting a stronger law. No, what I realized was that Lakeman was insisting on a more democratic process because she was certain that that was the only way we could do it right. In solidarity, we supported her.

"How many women do you want to invite?" asked Campbell. After a quick discussion, we decided that 200 would do it and that it could be done quickly, but not by Christmas. After the initial meeting with Campbell, the justice consultations took place once a year in Ottawa and covered a variety of justice issues, with a special emphasis on violence against women. Women representing different constituencies met in Ottawa, first with one another and then with the minister and justice officials, to lobby and provide advice. Not only did the minister get the benefit of the experience of grass-roots women's groups, but the women's groups got an unprecedented opportunity to meet together at the Canada-wide level and plan strategy. The justice consultations continued after Allan Rock became minister in 1993, but were cancelled by Anne McLellan in 1999.

The first consultation was incredibly productive. Because the group was so representative, we went beyond the usual arguments for this position or that. Decisions were also taken based on the individual experiences of members of the various groups. Every workshop had a lawyer, a representative from the initial consultation meeting with Campbell, and then a diverse sampling of women. Each woman learned what had happened in our meetings with Campbell and knew what the legal parameters were. Sometimes, women wanted to go beyond those parameters, and then the lawyers would try to figure out a way to do so. It was through these meetings that we developed the definition of the word "consent" that now appears in a somewhat modified form in the bill itself. We also decided to argue for a preamble, highly unusual in the Canadian Criminal Code, that would place the sexual-assault law in the context of equality rights and point out that some women were more vulnerable to assault and had less access to the justice system than others. In the end, we did not succeed in convincing Campbell to include the preamble. But just the discussion of it in a parliamentary committee ensured that it informed the Supreme Court decision that upheld the law so many years later.

Most of the women attending our workshop were activists in the anti-violence field. The women who would be affected directly by this law seemed like the appropriate people to be consulted, and the only way to reach them was through the groups they had already organized. The other interested parties, like the accused and the judicial system, were to be represented in the consultations by bureaucrats and politicians. Then a later parliamentary committee would hold hearings to get direct public input.

Parliamentary committees are about the only means citizens have for direct input into the policy-making process. In fact, these committees are the most direct and public way that citizens have to contribute to political decision making. One problem with them, however, is that ordinary citizens rarely attend. The people who present positions to these committees almost always have a particular interest. The committee then becomes the ground on which the opposite sides fight out their positions. Sometimes the committee will support one position over another; sometimes it will draft something in between and call it a compromise. In this case, women's groups would appear to fight for the law, with some modifications, and the defence bar would argue that it placed too heavy a burden on the accused.

Another problem with these committee hearings is that the parliamentarians usually have their own biases towards the groups presenting before them. During my years at NAC, a feminist organization that was almost always in opposition to the Conservative government, I rarely got a positive hearing from a parliamentary committee. As a result, NAC usually viewed my appearances before a parliamentary committee as more of a way to get media coverage than to persuade politicians. I remember only one parliamentary committee where I felt that I actually changed the minds of the members of Parliament present, and that was the Senate committee on abortion in 1990. The House of Commons had just passed a law re-criminalizing abortion, and the law had to get through the Senate before it could take effect. NAC presented a brief that we thought would get media coverage because it presented some new arguments on the pro-choice side. In this case, we didn't get media coverage, but we did get a very interested response from the senators. To this day, I remember looking around the committee room and seeing interested and curious faces instead of the usual barely disguised hostility or impatient tolerance. As it turned out, the Senate was preparing to overturn the House's decision on the law.

Parliamentary committee hearings are also problematic because cabinet ministers will often ignore their recommendations and develop the policy favoured by officials and lobbyists. But despite their limitations, these hearings are the only mechanism for direct and public citizen input into the decision-making process.

As a women's advocate, I always hoped that, whatever the legislation, those directly affected by it would have the greatest input. Unfortunately, the rape law experience, by virtue of its extraordinary nature, demonstrates that they rarely do. Too often, what is also missing is the input of disinterested citizens, the public, the people.

David Shulman thinks he knows how such input could be organized into the existing system. Shulman is the coordinator of a Canadian group called the Democracy Education Network, an alliance of educators concerned with promoting the skills of participatory democracy. He says that our current democratic process only gives citizens choices that have been developed by elite groups in society.

"There's lots of opportunity to express an opinion on this or that, or to join this group or another promoting a cause or an issue, but there is no space to find out what you think," Shulman told me in an interview. He favours study circles as a method of ensuring direct citizen input into the policy-making process. This is some-times called small group democracy. The idea is that citizens are organized into small groups to discuss a particular policy issue. While study circles are used extensively in countries such as Sweden, there has been only one in Canada. Shulman and his group organ-ized it for the federal government around the unlikely topic of immigration. If ever there was a topic where you might fear the input of the general public, it was this one.

"What the study-circle process revealed," explained Shulman, "is that whatever the Reform Party or the polls were saying, people were not against immigration. They were critical of immigration. What participants realized once they had the information was that immigration had been going up between 1984 and 1994 but [that] services and language training were being cut in the same period. The government had come up with a target of one percent immi-gration to try to calm the fears they found reflected in the polls. Our study circles said they should open to as much immigration as they could afford to integrate. [Participants] favoured immigration, but they wanted to make sure that the services could be available to settle immigrants in the country successfully." Pretty sensible.

Citizens participating in the immigration consultation were organized into groups of fifteen. Ads placed in community news-papers sought participants, and the organizers reached out to various community groups to ensure that the study circles would be fully representative. The circles included immigrants, native-born Canadians, and advocates and experts. Anyone who wanted to attend could just register, as if for a university course. In all, 1,200 people across the country signed up. "We wanted representa-tion that was diverse along income, race, and culture [lines]," said Shulman. "If MPs wanted to attend, we told them to leave the ini-tials at the door and participate as citizens. Our approach was to have experts on tap rather than experts on top, so we were a little wary of immigration lawyers."

Each participant got a package of material that included the

Liberals' Red Book, which had promised the one percent immigration target, and a document from the Department of Immigration outlining the history of immigration. "We told the officials, 'You can shape the way your department is portrayed in the materials, but you cannot have editorial control.'" Professional teachers and facilitators edited the documents to make sure they did not present a particular bias. The package also included worksheets; an introduction to the history of immigration policy; information about what countries immigrants most often come from; facts about who is responsible for various policies and services; and a paper that presented the arguments on the different sides of the immigration debate. Participants received the material in advance and were expected to prepare for the study circle. A willingness to prepare in this way was the only pre-requisite of the study circles.

"When we came up with the idea," says Shulman, "a lot of advocates and bureaucrats were worried that the neo-fascists would try to stack some of the meetings. I said, 'Don't worry. Neo-fascists aren't interested in participating in a meeting for which they have to study.' And they didn't participate."

Childcare was provided to participants, and every event was fully accessible. "It is key, if we are to develop a culture of democracy, that we bring the kids along," says Shulman. "My own experience came from my dad. My brother was aphasic and deaf, and I remember my dad fighting for special education. That's probably why I became an activist." Childcare is also essential to ensuring the involvement of women.

The study circles opened with the facilitators asking people in the room to tell their stories and their experiences with immigration. This is a standard popular-education technique: people learn best from their own experiences. In this case, there was the added value of grounding the policy discussion in the experiences of actual immigrants. Three questions were then put to each individual in the group: What do I think? Why do I think what I think? Why would someone else think differently? Facilitators also made sure that everyone participated.

The first thing that surprised Shulman was how few regional differences there were. This was a realization that had surprised me during the pre–Charlottetown Accord meetings as well. Supporters of decentralizing federal power would have us believe that regionalism or provincialism is increasing in Canada. And of course, the premiers have a vested interest in arguing from the perspective of their individual provinces. But citizens argue from their own experiences, only a small part of which is about living in a particular province.

"I was amazed that even in the heart of Alberta, when people discovered that Quebec had different immigration powers than the other provinces, it made sense to them," said Shulman. "No one had a problem with it. When they looked at the figures about who was coming from which countries, the arguments about the good old days, when the majority of immigrants came from Europe, just disappeared. No one [is applying] to come from the British Isles and Northern Europe any more. What's the point of talking about it?"

The study-circle process, says Shulman, is a way to really talk about an issue in all its complexity. He says we never have an opportunity to discuss the pros and cons of a certain issue. We are invited to choose sides in a highly polarized debate, but we are never asked to give an informed opinion ourselves. The closest we get are polls, which are very far away from mature reflection. Another factor in study circles, which was also true in those constitutional conferences leading up to the Charlottetown Accord, is that the usual power inequalities in society are removed to the greatest extent possible. The average citizen has as much access to public space as the politician or the media commentator. Instead of one side having access to almost all the media, both sides are presented even-handedly. In a society where elites dominate public debate, professionally facilitated study groups or workshops can make a lot of difference.

Unlike study groups, polls are little more than a snapshot of public opinion. Their accuracy depends on how they are done. In his 1991 book *Coming to Public Judgment*, the American public-opinion expert Daniel Yankelovich explains that polls can produce very different results depending on the questions they ask. "When people were asked in an NBC News/Associated Press poll about their opinion of a constitutional amendment to require the federal government to balance its budget, a 64 percent majority said they approved," Yankelovich wrote. "Yet, as soon as people learned that such an amendment might result in higher taxes, the 64 percent majority, as if by magic, shrank to a 39 percent minority." He also gives the example of an NBC News/*Wall Street Journal* poll that showed that 51 percent favoured "greater limits on foreign imports in the interests of protecting American jobs. When the same people were told that such restrictions might affect the variety and choice available to consumers, only 41 percent supported them. When they were told prices might be higher, support for protectionism dropped to 36 percent."

In other words, if you take a poll asking people whether they want higher taxes, they will of course say no. If, however, you ask whether they would be willing to pay higher taxes to ensure universal health care or quality care for children, most will say yes. In this book, I use a lot of polling information from Ekos Research. The results of Ekos polls are often quite different from poll results you read in the business press, partly because Ekos is asking different questions. Ekos has also done two in-depth surveys comparing the opinions of elite decision-makers with those of the general public. Finally, because Ekos tracks opinion over time, I think its polls provide a more accurate picture than the snapshot we get with most polls. But of course, I also select the polls that best support my point of view, just as politicians and the mainstream media do.

Polling experts like Eleanor Singer, the former president of the American Association of Public Opinion Research, point out the numerous problems with polls: people do not always reply truthfully; most poll questions are too simple to reflect the richness of people's experiences; sometimes people don't understand certain types of questions; survey researchers tend to impose their own framework on the public; people will give an opinion even if they don't have one; and people answer differently depending on the context. So polls are a very limited basis upon which to judge public opinion. At best, they are simply an accurate snapshot of public opinion at one moment in time. Citizen forums like David Shulman's study circles are a deeper and more accurate reflection of public opinion.

Citizen forums are not new to Canada. There was broad public discussion in the 1940s, for example, when Paul Martin, Sr., put forward the 1947 Canadian Citizenship Act, which defined Canadian citizenship for the first time. CBC Radio broadcast much of the discussion, and citizens used the public broadcaster as a means to reach other citizens across the country. Two decades earlier, Canadians had seen another type of citizen forum in the Antigonish Movement. This movement, first developed in Nova Scotia in the 1920s by Father Moses Coady and Father Jimmy Tompkins, focused on adult education as a means to social improvement. A member of the movement would enter a community and make contact with as many people as possible. Then he or she would call a meeting and facilitate a discussion of the community's needs. A study club would be created, and at the end of a series of public meetings, a co-operative or two would be organized to meet the needs identified.

The co-op movement spread across the country in the 1930s and 1940s and took deep root in Saskatchewan. Today, institutional co-ops suffer from the same plague of elitism and bureaucratization as other large institutions, but the co-op movement nevertheless remains one of the most important areas of citizen activism. During the 1940s, the movement became internationally known through a series of books and articles; indeed, it was a training ground for thousands of community organizers from around the world.

According to David Shulman, we have all the infrastructure we need to fully implement a study-circle democracy in Canada. Schools are ideal locations for citizen study groups in every community to meet. The Internet can be used to distribute study-group kits inexpensively and to provide a forum for interactive feedback by the general public. Every citizen could be informed of the study circles through regular government mailings. Each individual study circle could nominate representatives to municipal, provincial, and then Canada-wide study circles. CBC Radio and/or Newsworld could broadcast the circles' deliberations, thus allowing the entire country to share the experience of those citizens who were participating directly in the political process. "The possibilities for democracy are enormous," says Shulman.

The study-group concept has won a lot of support among Ottawa mandarins. They call it citizen engagement. It was for a conference on the topic that Ekos conducted its survey *Rethinking Citizen Engagement*. Forty-five percent of the 2,000 respondents to that survey said that the federal government consults Canadians badly on major issues; only 24 percent thought the feds consulted well. Eighty-seven percent of respondents also said the government should place more emphasis on consulting, and 77 percent agreed with the statement, "Today's citizens are better educated and informed and should have more say in decisions." In comparison, these two questions were answered positively by 66 percent and 57 percent of decision-makers. Only 35 percent of the general public thought that citizens didn't have the time or knowledge needed to offer useful advice to the government on complex issues, and as I mentioned earlier, fully 69 percent felt that most big national problems could be solved at the grass-roots level.

The survey next asked, "Would you participate in an engagement exercise . . . if it meant a one-hour meeting per month, publicly presenting your views, and two hours of document review every other weekend?" Seventy percent said they would participate in such an engagement exercise on improved services for children and families, 59 percent on redesigning the social safety net, and 57 percent in setting immigration levels. When asked to rank the principles of engagement, 37 percent thought representing the views of the general public was most important, 28 percent chose reflecting the basic values of Canadians, 23 percent selected listening to those who know the most about the issues, and 12 percent wanted to reflect the views of those who take the time to get involved.

It seems, then, that there can be little doubt that study circles would enormously increase public participation in the political process, and that would be a step forward. There are, however, a number of problems.

First, if the study groups were to get any power in the system, the various groups would likely try to stack them and they would become more like parliamentary committee hearings. The organized takeover of hospital boards by anti-abortion activists demonstrates that instruments of local democracy can always be diverted by dedicated, committed activists for one issue or another. On the other hand, the fact that no other groups have tried to do the same thing (for example, with school boards) indicates that most organizations respect the democratic process when it is fairly administered. Some might argue that the study groups would be even more representative if they were elected. For example, each workplace in a neighbourhood could elect a delegate and perhaps community organizations like the PTA, the small business persons group, and the local women's shelter could also send delegates. Perhaps one-third of the spots could be saved for self-registered participants, as long as they were demographically representative. In any case, the potential for a dramatic increase in citizen participation is indeed enormous.

A second potential problem is that once the study groups had power, facilitators would be pressured to favour the government's views. If even one Canada-wide study group came up with solutions opposed by the government in power, the process would almost certainly be either stopped or manipulated. On the other hand, if study-circle democracy was to become a regular feature of our democratic process — like the court system, for example — a culture of independence enforced by laws could develop.

The most obvious problem is choosing who makes the decisions. The pre-Charlottetown conferences were a much more public, much more expensive mechanism of consultation than study groups, and still their recommendations were almost completely ignored by the politicians making the final decision. "Getting people into dialogue is easy," says Shulman, "compared to getting receptivity on the other side." He recommends a series of measures, including requiring government departments to disclose to what extent public dialogue influenced their decisions.

The fourth problem is that unless direct citizenship involvement is formally structured into the system, as it is in Brazil, then the elitist, partisan habits of the existing system would likely corrupt the independence of the study groups. Real active citizenship would have to involve real decision-making power. It cannot just be an add-on to a bureaucratic, hierarchical system. It has to change the system.

At the moment, the most powerful players in the political arena are the prime minister and his staff, senior cabinet ministers and their staffs, senior government bureaucrats, lobbyists, and the media/pollsters. The ministers, and more and more the prime minister and the finance minister, make their decisions based more on options defined and determined by the senior bureaucrats who consult with lobbyists than on parliamentary debates and House of Commons question periods. Most attention is paid to those lobbyists who represent corporate interests — unless the pollsters or the media tell the bureaucrats that they should be worrying about a group without much power.

That's pretty well how the system works. When it works well, usually on an issue that doesn't interest the corporate elite, the senior bureaucrats make an effort to find out what will be in the best interests of the people affected by the policy in question and the media pay attention to the various advocacy groups. When it works badly, it is a secretive, closed process that responds to the needs of the economic elite and is governed only by polls that tell the government what it can get away with. The study-group process would help to shine some light on this secrecy.

A further problem, according to Shulman, is that the study

groups will have their agendas set by the government. In other words, only the government will decide which issues are important enough to put out for dialogue. Shulman thinks there should also be citizen-initiated policies.

There has to be some way of judging which issues are important enough to merit inclusion in the study-circle process. Unfortunately, we know how to do this only through government or bureaucratic decision, or by collecting the support of enough citizens on a petition. The problem with the first method is that it leaves the power over important issues with the same people who ignored them in the first place. Getting government to focus on an issue would require just as much lobbying and organizing as getting an issue on the agenda already does. And the problem with the second method is that the well-organized and well-resourced interest groups would be the ones most likely to get their petitions signed.

A lot of people on the left are wary of direct democratic processes because of the way right-wing forces have used them in California and other American states to get room on the ballot for their pet issues. Defeating reactionary citizen initiatives can divert a lot of energy from pursuing progressive policies, it's true. But surely this requires no more energy than policing a reactionary government that does the same things without nearly the same level of debate and public education. If it means the full participation of every citizen who wants to participate, then I have enough confidence in my ideas to risk the more democratic arena every time.

Most people on the left prefer to rely on organized groups; they take clear and usually democratic policy decisions based on the experiences, interests, and opinions of their members. In fact, advocacy groups, citizen groups, and unions are among the most democratically organized institutions in our society. Their role is to represent a particular interest, however broad, and this is an incredibly important part of the democratic process, especially to those who are not present at the tables of power. Here is another area where elite opinion as reflected in the media is quite different from public opinion. In that familiar Ekos survey, fully 90 percent of respondents felt it was important for citizens to participate in voluntary organizations; 51 percent said they were likely to work through a group, while only 42 percent said they would contact the media and 29 percent said they would work through a political party. Sixty-eight percent thought community groups should have more power.

The inclusion of advocacy groups in the political process was one of the major contributions of the 1960s movements. The participation at a grass-roots level of a wide variety of groups representing the interests of their members has deepened democracy in fundamental ways. The problem is that such groups have since been integrated, to a greater or lesser degree, into the existing system. And since almost all the power still rests at the top, we can conclude that they have not succeeded in transforming that system. In fact, one could argue that the corporate elite, in response to the challenge of these movements, has grown ever more dominant, and that political parties have centralized power in the hands of a few clever backroom operators who control contact with the public.

In the end, the role of advocacy groups is to advocate for the interests of their members. They are always arguing for governments to implement their proposals, and governments are usually arguing that they can't or that they'll have to think about it. Dialogue rarely happens. By their very nature, advocacy groups are not in a position to look at competing interests and judge how to accommodate them. At the moment, it is politicians and bureaucrats who make these kinds of decisions. But as we shall see, they are not necessarily made with the interests of the people directly affected in mind. In fact, even when those in power intend to meet the interests of the people, their social situation does not always allow them an understanding of what those interests might be.

Study circles could be a powerful expression of active citizenship. If, however, study circles are simply grafted onto the existing system, they will be manipulated the way opinion polls are manipulated. As the Brazilian Workers Party has learned, participatory democracy works only when citizens see that their work is affecting political decisions. Study circles should be one element of active citizenship. The other elements, which are described in the following chapters, are also necessary to ensure the development of a culture of democracy that can resist corruption and manipulation.

6

A Referendum on Referendums

Just before I was elected president of NAC in the spring of 1990, a *Toronto Star* reporter who was doing a profile of me said, "You've been involved in the very polarized debate on abortion. It's so un-Canadian to be that polarized." I pointed out to her that politics were changing in Canada. Both the Meech Lake and free trade debates were as polarized, if not quite as passionate, as the abortion debate. Yet in 1990, journalists still bought into the mythology of a compliant populace that might complain now and then but basically went along with whatever the politicians decided.

That fall, the Spicer Commission began to change that perception by giving Canadians a chance to voice their grievances. The referendum on the Charlottetown Accord, in the fall of 1992, was another wake-up call, a shocking (to the elites) illustration of how wide and deep the fury really was. And then the 1993 election reduced a once-powerful ruling party, the Progressive Conservatives, to a rump and placed close to power a party full of rednecks, the Reform Party. This finally convinced the elites that something was happening, even if it was not exactly clear what it was.

In a few short years, the Reform Party has gone from fringe party to official opposition largely on the strength of its populism. A lot of voters supported Reformers over Tories no doubt because of their fiscal conservatism. One of the most interesting features of the 1993 election, however, was the number of votes Reformers earned in former NDP ridings in British Columbia. Unlike many members of the B.C. NDP, Bill Tieleman, one of the architects of Glen Clark's election victory, thinks that a lot of federal NDP votes went to Reform because Reform replaced the NDP as the anti-establishment party. Ron Johnson, president of Now Communications and another B.C. NDP strategist, says the move from NDP to Reform in the last two federal elections occurred mainly in rural areas and was related to populism.

Yet most NDPers would rather think of these ex-NDPers as rednecks than acknowledge that there is a problem with the way their party behaves in the democratic arena. Jumping into bed with the hated Mulroney Tories, as the federal NDP did over the Charlottetown Accord, was probably the worst blow to the party's credibility as a voice for the ordinary person. The campaign in favour of the accord was one of the worst examples of elite politics we have ever seen in this country. The Yes side arrogantly refused to take seriously the growing public opposition to the accord. Instead of responding to people's concerns with rational arguments, Yes supporters issued threats. At various times, members of the Yes side, including the prime minister, threatened that the country would fall apart and that there would be an economic crisis if the accord was defeated. But in their minds the accord never would be defeated, because they believed no one of any importance in political circles opposed it.

Everywhere I spoke, people would thank me for responding to their questions in a serious manner and treating them like intelligent beings. I can only assume that most speakers from the Yes side were pretty patronizing. Certainly the Yes ads were an insult to the intelligence of their opponents.

Gerry Kaplan, who represented the NDP on the Yes strategy

committee, once told me that his fellow committee members were so arrogant and out of touch that they were completely unwilling to recognize their loss of support. Even in the last days of the referendum campaign, they clung to the belief that they would win. Ironically, their incredible arrogance, along with the hated Mulroney's, ensured that they would lose.

Ekos Research president Frank Graves told me that he had tested different forms of ballots during Charlottetown. His tests showed that when people were given a ballot where they could indicate yes or no on each section of the accord and then vote yes or no on the entire agreement, the yes vote was 10 to 12 percent higher. If a different ballot had been used, in other words, the Yes side could very well have won the referendum. Graves says, "They didn't use the longer ballot because the premier of Alberta [Don Getty] was worried that it would show that the majority of people in Alberta didn't agree with the Triple-E Senate, and that would be embarrassing for him." Graves's view is that if people had had the chance to say what it was they didn't like about the accord, they would have been more likely to give it their overall approval. The Yes side risked losing the entire accord so that no one would be embarrassed by really knowing what people didn't like about it.

This all reminds me of a story. When I first moved out of my parents' house in a suburb of Montreal in 1967, I lived with an older man in a tiny apartment downtown. My parents moved to Toronto later that year and were coming to visit. Needless to say, in 1967 you didn't tell your parents you were living with a man if you weren't married, and so I was very nervous about their impending trip. My friend Peter Marcovitz said, "Don't worry, Judy. If Ruth sees two toothbrushes in the bathroom, is she going to ask Jack, 'Jack, why do you suppose there are two toothbrushes in the bathroom?' Is Jack going to ask Ruth, 'Ruth, why are there two toothbrushes in the bathroom?' They won't ask because they don't want to know why there are two toothbrushes in the bathroom."

Peter was a wise man, and he proved to be right. My parents didn't want to know because they knew there was nothing they could do about it if they did know. Our leaders are faced with the same dilemma. They don't want to know what we think and what we want in case it goes against what they think is best for us. Sounds silly, but in a way I think it is true. The arrogance of elite rule is that the elites think they know better than the people.

This is one reason for the opposition to integrating referendums into our democratic process. It was during the auto-insurance debacle in Ontario that I first started to think about referendums. One of the most popular promises of Bob Rae's NDP government in Ontario was that it would introduce public auto insurance. This had been central to the party's election platform for several campaigns before the 1990 win. In fact, public auto insurance had been a signature issue for both the NDP and the CCF since the 1940s. When I ran provincially for the NDP in 1987, it was the central issue in that campaign. Three NDP-run provinces and Quebec, under the PQ, had already shown that a public monopoly in auto insurance could significantly lower the cost of premiums. In fact, public auto insurance was so popular that even subsequent right-wing governments in these provinces didn't privatize the public insurance schemes.

In 1989, the Liberal government in Ontario under David Peterson had flirted with public auto insurance, but the party, under massive pressure from the insurance industry, opted instead for a no-fault system that took away the right of accident victims to sue. This system saved the insurance industry a fortune, and in return insurance companies agreed to moderate their rates. In the 1990 election, Bob Rae promised to reverse the no-fault provisions as a first step and then to provide public auto insurance as a second step. Unfortunately, it was not to be.

According to the *Toronto Star* journalist Tom Walkom, in his book *Rae Days*, members of the auto-insurance industry were not the only ones against public auto insurance. "Bureaucrats within the Ministry of Financial Institutions were uneasy about the NDP plans," Walkom wrote. "They had already been through this exercise once with the Liberals and felt that the NDP dream was hope-lessly naive." Walkom then describes the various machinations of elite politics that eventually forced the NDP to retreat from the proposal, thus breaking their most important promise to the voters.

It was my view at the time, and has been ever since, that if Rae had called a referendum on auto insurance, even if it had not been binding, he could have used the results to subdue both the industry and the bureaucrats. Citizen support for public auto insurance was at 85 percent in polls at the time, and there is no doubt that Rae would have won a massive victory in such a referendum. This not only would have forced the insurance industry to back off, it would have put everyone else in corporate Ontario on notice that the Rae government would go to the people if they started bullying him, as they managed to do very successfully in the next few years.

But using referendums as a way of mobilizing public opinion only when it is on your side is not really very democratic. If we are to opt for referendums, they should be available for any major issue that either elected politicians or a significant number of citizens believe is worth putting to a vote.

Parliamentary democracies have been loath to use referendums as a mechanism of direct citizen participation. Many argue that ref-erendums interfere with the work of our representatives. Of course, the idea of representative democracy is that we elect our betters to represent us. Yet the original idea of democracy was that every cit-izen had an equal voice in deciding how to be governed. In a cover story in *The Economist* in December 1996, Brian Beedham called our version of democracy part-time democracy. "The defenders of the old-fashioned form of democracy," he wrote, "have to face the fact that the world has changed radically since the time when it might have seemed plausible to think the voters' wishes needed to be fil-tered through the finer intelligence of those representatives."

Politicians, because they make the decisions, have a self-interest in limiting the forms of participatory democracy. So since the system itself refuses to change, citizens have found their own ways to have a say more often than every four or five years. Community groups, citizens' groups, advocacy groups, and business groups have organized and provide for citizens a voice in the policy-making process that has been indispensable. When such groups can mobilize enough popular support, or convince the media or some powerful politicians of the importance of their issue, they can have an important influence on public policy. But as we have seen in the past ten years, groups that are powerful at one time in history can be marginalized at another time. Unions, for example, played a much more powerful political role in the 1940s and 1950s than they do today. Women's groups were more prominent in the 1980s, which is also when environmental groups were in their heyday. Today right-wing think-tanks like the Fraser and C. D. Howe institutes seem to set the political agenda. Hopefully, they too will soon be marginalized.

Because direct democracy can be such an effective force, I am always astonished by how strongly many members of the left oppose it. "What about California?" opponents will always say. In California, citizens have the right to put any propositions they choose on the ballot if they get enough signatures on a petition. Since 1970, voters have approved forty-five such initiatives. For $200, you can present an idea to the state's attorney-general, whose office will draft a brief summary and give it a title. After that, you need to get the valid signatures of 433,269 voters, and this is an expensive undertaking. In fact, because it's so expensive and time-consuming, most people think that the initiatives are used primarily by powerful right-wing special interests. This is a valid concern that could be addressed by providing public funding for both sides. Yet in California, the evidence is that large spending by special-interest groups does not guarantee the passage of a measure. Elisabeth Gerber, of the University of California at San Diego, has found that wealthy special-interest groups such as the oil and tobacco industries almost never succeed in pushing through self-serving initiatives. This is true even a little closer to home: during the debate over the Charlottetown Accord, the Yes side spent ten times as much money as the No side.

One argument in favour of referendums is that big money can now buy decisions in the backrooms, where their lobbyists are not always required to argue their position openly and subject it to the light of democratic dialogue and debate. Referendums are much more favourable terrain for those without economic and political power. Even in controversial California, the labour movement was able to defeat Proposition 226, which sought to force unions to get written annual permission from each member before spending their dues on political campaigns. They defeated the proposition through a massive mobilization of union members, who were able to explain to the people of California that this was a direct attack on the democracy of their own organizations. The legalization of the medical use of marijuana was won through a similar citizens' initiative, an amazing achievement in a country that has forced the entire world to continue the incredibly harmful war on drugs. In 1974, California voters overruled the resistance of interest groups to pass Proposition 9, which set some firm spending limits on referendum campaigns. Unfortunately, this proposition was quashed by the Supreme Court in the name of freedom of speech.

Of course, we cannot ignore the fact that there have been some reactionary initiatives passed in California, including the "three strikes law," which gives life in prison to anyone convicted of a criminal offence three times, and Proposition 187, which sought to deny public services to illegal immigrants. People on the left always point to these reactionary decisions in their arguments against direct democracy. But are the people any more reactionary than their representatives? I don't think so. In a referendum, at least both sides have the opportunity to argue their cases before the people. During the debate over the Charlottetown Accord, I found the media fairer in covering both sides than I have ever seen except during elections. Even though the No side had only two recognizable media spokespeople in English Canada, me and Preston Manning, the media were scrupulous in giving equal coverage to the two sides.

In any case, voters can set the rules under which referendums take place to ensure equal access. They can even decide to provide equal public funding for both sides of a referendum, as they do in Quebec. There could be three phases of citizen initiative. One phase would require an interest group to collect a certain number of signatures to become eligible for funding for the campaign to get a proposition on the ballot. The next phase would be to collect the number of signatures required to get on the ballot, and the final phase would be the referendum campaign itself. All three phases could be funded by public money, or at the very least interest groups could be given the same access to tax deductions as political parties have.

Perhaps the best place to look at how this kind of direct democracy works is Switzerland, where it has been practised for years. According to *The Economist's* Brian Beedham, "The first lesson from Switzerland is that direct democracy is hard work. The second is that, though it makes politicians less important than they like to be, it does not remove the need for an intelligent parliament; the system works most efficiently when politicians stop assuming they know best and do their proper job with modest zeal."

Politicians in Switzerland do the same things politicians in other countries do. The difference is that in Switzerland, the citizens may have the last word. Fifty thousand signatures, a little more than one percent of the qualified voters, is enough to bring a new countrywide law before a vote of the whole populace. Twice that number of signatures is required to put a brand-new idea to the people — even if Parliament wants nothing to do with it. Almost 450 questions have gone to a national referendum vote since the current system got going about 130 years ago. That's about three and a half per year, although it has been accelerating lately.

The Swiss decide on a wide variety of issues. In 1993, a group of signature collectors who wanted to stop the Swiss airforce from buying new fighter aircraft and also wanted to reduce the number of bases the army is allowed to use came within a few percentage points of winning its case. And before that, the voters decided against joining the European Economic Union — against the advice of almost all of their leaders. Yet most of the laws written by Parliament that have been put to a referendum have passed and nine-tenths of the proposals put forward by citizens' groups have been defeated.

According to Beedham, "If anything, people and Parliament get on better these days than they used to; only about a quarter of the acts of Parliament put to the referendum since 1960 have been rejected, compared with well over half 100 years ago." Beedham goes on to explain that "there is a solid basis of partnership between the politicians of Switzerland and the people with their special power. The voters are content to let the politicians do most of the routine work of politics and to listen to their advice on many complicated issues. The politicians, for their part, have learned that ordinary people are often surprisingly (to politicians) shrewd in their decisions."

In Switzerland, voters have refused to be frightened by anti-immigrant propaganda into sending home foreign workers; in the 1980s and 1990s, they were persuaded to start paying a value-added tax. "Not long ago," says Beedham, "there was a splendid moment after most of the political class had shaken a furious fist at the voters' refusal to accept an anti-urban-sprawl planning law. The politicians then discovered that just as much sprawl could be prevented more cheaply and by a different scheme. Politicians and people may occasionally snarl at each other, but they have learned to work together."

Many people argue that the biggest problem with referendums is that they afford little protection of minority rights. Indeed, it is hard to imagine that gays and lesbians, for example, would have been able to make the gains they have made in the past ten years through a referendum process. But then we mustn't forget that most of these gains were made through the courts because the politicians were too craven to pass any legislation that went beyond simple protection against discrimination. Constitutional protection of

99

minority rights through the courts would hold just as fast in a participatory democracy as in a representative one. The rule of law and constitutional protections would still apply. Voters could not deny minority rights any more easily than governments can.

People often hold up native land claims in B.C. as another example of an issue that might have ended with a more negative result through a referendum than through representative democracy. I am not so sure. Consider how long aboriginal people have put up with the paternalism of governments and how long it has taken them to get self-government on the agenda. Perhaps a viable referendum rule would have given aboriginal people a route other than the courts to win their rights from governments. And as in the gay and lesbian rights case, the courts would still arbitrate constitutional issues, which would mean that those minority rights that are already enshrined in the charter would be unassailable. There could also be issues of minority rights that would be constitutionally excluded from the referendum process. Perhaps a minority group or a government could demand a court reference on an initiative that appeared to be denying minority rights.

An equally vexing problem is how to ensure the participation of marginalized people in the referendum process. Whether they've been marginalized because of social class, income, or race, there are people in every democracy who vote less often and participate less fully in the life of the community. Unfortunately, there is little evidence that the referendum process mobilizes such groups. In fact, Beedham argues that such people fare even worse in referendums than they do in elections. Statistics from all over the world, he points out, show that participation in referendums is almost always a bit lower than participation in elections. And the lower the turnout, the worse minorities perform. Studies in the U.S. and Switzerland show that as turnout declines, the proportion of the vote cast by the poor drops even further. "Referendums are a more middle-class way of doing things than parliamentary elections," observes Beedham.

The challenge here is to develop other forms of direct democracy that will involve poor and marginalized people much more in the affairs of the state, especially those that directly affect them. By getting more involved in government decisions, marginalized people will get more involved in the general public debate. I have seen it happen all my life. When someone joins a women's group or an anti-poverty group, that person, rather than becoming stuck in an area of narrow self-interest (as politicians would like us to believe), grows more interested in politics overall. If you feel that you have an influence on public policy on one level, it is much more likely that you will develop an interest in public policy on other levels. Most of the cynicism and passivity we see today in relation to politics has to do with the feeling that nothing anyone does will make any difference. The challenge of active citizenship is for citizens to learn they really can make a difference.

Unlike the relatively new idea of study groups, which I discussed in the last chapter, there has been considerable debate about using referendums and citizen initiatives in Canada. Most of the support for referendums in Canada has come from the right, which makes them suspect in the eyes of a lot of progressive people. The Reform Party proposes holding referendums on what they call moral questions, such as abortion and capital punishment. I don't know why these questions are considered any more moral than cutting the poor off welfare or slashing social spending instead of raising taxes, but I have no problem with any matter of major public policy going to referendum.

Capital punishment is the one issue that most people use to argue against referendums. The majority of Canadians still seem to support capital punishment, although politicians have thankfully refused to re-implement it. While it wouldn't be on the top of my list of issues that should go to referendum, I am certain that a full public debate on the matter would result in its defeat. I also think there are few today in the country who would see the issue as being of sufficient importance to organize a national petition campaign on the subject.

Of course, the biggest problem with referendums is that it's possible to have too many of them. As Brian Beedham points out, the more we call referendums, especially those based on questions posed by what he calls "excited groups of enthusiasts," the fewer people will vote. The requirements for placing a referendum question on the ballot should be stringent enough that only one or two questions a year will be placed before the populace. Another way of restricting the number of referendums is to amend the constitution to outline what kinds of questions politicians are required to put to a public vote. This is a less attractive method than allowing citizen initiatives — especially in Canada, where amending the constitution is such a difficult process — but it would be an improvement over the current situation, where politicians can use referendums to further their own ends.

The worst example of this comes from the Mike Harris government in Ontario, probably the least democratic government we have ever seen in Canada. Harris and his cronies refuse to even consult with groups they disagree with. They centralized education, which used to be the most democratically delivered of the social services, despite strenuous opposition from parents, teachers, and school boards. They control Queen's Park with an iron hand, dictating to bureaucrats what their key issues are and refusing to even look at any other policy directions. And to top it all off, Harris passed legislation that requires a referendum before future governments can raise taxes; this is mainly a device to stop these governments from changing what he has done.

Right-wing supporters of direct democracy often include recall as part of their proposals. They want citizens to be able to remove their MPs between elections. Recall, or impeachment, may make sense in a congressional system, but it makes no sense in a parliamentary system, where governments can be sent to the polls by non-confidence votes or effective parliamentary and public opposition. Also, given that individual MPs have so little power in the parliamentary system, recalling one seems like a foolish waste of time. Even more seriously, since in our first-past-the-post electoral system few MPs get elected with a majority of votes, any coalition of opposition parties could get enough signatures to demand a recall vote. It undermines our electoral system to allow the possibility of being recalled by a majority when you can be elected by a minority. As I argue in a later chapter, I believe the electoral system would be more democratic if it was based on proportional representation, but even in this system few MPs would be elected by majority vote.

Recall is a way of channelling voter anger, but it is no solution to it. If voters were more involved in the decision-making process to begin with, they would be less interested in recalling the people they elect to Parliament. In other words, to effectively deal with voter anger we have to create a culture of participatory democracy, and referendums are but one part of that culture.

Of course, citizen engagement through study groups, town-hall meetings, and referendums still deals only with the opinion side of the political equation. That leaves us with the implementation of political decisions. Can we democratize the institutions that deliver services to us?

7

PARTICIPATORY ADMINISTRATION

THERE HAS BEEN PRECIOUS LITTLE DISCUSSION in government about how to democratize the administration of the state, mainly because state administration is practically invisible to the public. When we think of politics, we think of elections and policy debate and legislation, but the implementation of decisions has as much or more impact on our lives than these.

Two recent examples of the price we pay for bureaucratic administration are the disasters in the fisheries on both coasts and the near-decimation of the nursing profession, which provoked a new militancy among nursing unions. Democratizing the administration of public policy could have avoided both calamities.

In the summer of 1998, I hosted an episode of CBC Radio's "Cross Country Checkup" on the fisheries. Images of angry citizens confronting the politicians whose decisions had destroyed their lives or their livelihoods were being broadcast quite frequently on our television sets that summer. Newfoundland fishery workers screamed in protest against the federal ministers who held a press conference to reveal the new fishery package. When the politicians announced there would be fifteen minutes for questions, one fishery worker shot back, "Fifteen minutes is all you've got for destroying our lives!" Pierre Pettigrew, who was human resources minister at the time, looked dazed and confused as he left the press conference under armed guard. I guess he was wondering why the people whose way of life had been destroyed weren't more grateful for the $730-million package of support.

On the other coast, where conservation measures to protect coho salmon might have put two-thirds of the fishing fleet out of business, fishers were just as angry. One spokesperson for the West Coast fishers called Ottawa's new conservation rules "a scorched earth policy." In fact, fishers from both coasts who called in to "Checkup" that day had the same story to tell. Ottawa doesn't listen to us, they complained. Newfoundlanders said the politicians wouldn't listen years ago when fishers told them the stocks were disappearing, and they still wouldn't listen today to suggested solutions. In B.C., fishers also felt their suggestions were falling on deaf ears.

The crisis of the fisheries is the canary in the globalization mineshaft, an early warning we can't afford to ignore. When big corporations are allowed to scoop up everything they want to make a profit, they can leave environmental and community devastation in their wake. The loss of the fishery in Newfoundland is not just one more example of downsizing, as some would have us believe; it is the destruction of a way of life that has sustained the people in coastal towns and villages for generations.

When restructuring happens in the fishery, it is the small fishers who are driven out of business. Ecologically and sociologically, this makes no sense. The so-called Mifflin buyout (named after former fisheries minister Fred Mifflin), which was designed to restructure the West Coast fishery, reduced fishing licences by 35 percent in 1996 without reducing fishing capacity at all. Corporate-owned and city-based seine boats scoop up all the fish and the small-scale fishers based in coastal villages are forced to get out of their life's work.

Do we, as a society, want to destroy this way of life on both coasts? Neo-conservative pundits tell us that it's passé to even ask such a question. "Let the market decide" is their mantra. But the market favours bigger and bigger corporations making more and more money. When it comes to the environment, that means devastation; when it comes to small, self-employed fishers, it means poverty and dependence; and when it comes to fishery workers, it means unemployment.

The anger and frustration of fishers on both coasts come from an intense feeling of powerlessness. One of the most powerful myths in our society is that if we work hard enough and well enough, we can provide for ourselves and our families. But of course, this isn't always the case. As the forces of savage capitalism deepen their greedy, destructive path, more and more people will find themselves in similar situations to the Newfoundland fishers. If we continue to worship market forces at the expense of the needs of our people, we will lose more of what makes Canada unique and appealing.

Scientists have been warning the Department of Fisheries about the danger of the disappearance of the cod stock since the 1960s. Newfoundlanders have been sounding the warning about rapacious foreign fishing fleets for years. Instead of dragging its feet for fear of the political consequences, Ottawa should have called a representative meeting of fishers, their union leaders, provincial politicians, and perhaps concerned conservationists to discuss the scientists' concerns. The people most involved could then have had the benefit of the scientific knowledge that the government had, and everyone could have begun discussing solutions instead of leaving it until it was too late. No doubt the result would have been better for the long-term survival of the fishery and the communities in Newfoundland.

Another example of the undemocratic nature of state administration is the crisis in nursing. During 1999, the country saw a wave of militant struggles, with nurses in both Saskatchewan and Quebec going out on popularly supported illegal strikes, defying back-to-work legislation. Deficit-driven health-care cuts had hit nurses first and hardest. As usual, those with the power in the system, the doctors and the hospital administrators, made sure that their pockets remained well-padded, then started chopping from the bottom up.

In every province, nurses faced layoffs, casualization, and wage freezes. The blow to the nursing profession was so great that enrolment in nursing schools declined dramatically. As a result of layoffs and attrition, the average age of nurses is now forty-seven; only 5 percent of nurses are under thirty. Nurses are fighting for the very survival of their profession, and by extension, for the survival of quality health-care services. Anyone who has ever been in the hospital knows how central nurses are to the health-care system. With an increase in home care for the growing elderly population, nurses will become even more important.

No one consulted the nurses when drastic cuts were made, so they used the only power they had, their unions, to make their voices heard. Today, as money goes back into the system, nurses want to make sure it is spent on the services that really matter to patients. Like the Ontario teachers who went out in the fall of 1998 on a two-week political strike, nurses in 1999 demonstrated that public-sector workers are the best defenders of our social programs.

Now imagine that instead of just reducing money to hospitals and allowing administrators to cut as they saw fit, governments brought together representative administrators, doctors, nurses, and hospital workers with a group representing hospital users. In such a forum, the nurses would have had a much better hearing than they had with their hospital administrators. Such a representative group might have decided to make the cuts somewhere other than at the bottom, and the nursing crisis could have been avoided. In setting up local health boards that make such decisions, some governments have already gone this route. The secret here is to make sure that these boards do not simply replicate the elite rule we have in our present system, but instead draw from a truly representative segment of the community. We also need to ensure that they have access to expert medical opinion on the health-care system but are not dominated by those experts.

Much of government administration is made up of boards, agencies, and commissions that are staffed primarily through patronage appointments. Every once in a while, there is a scandal about patronage, but in fact it is central to our entire political system. Understandably, given the way our system is structured, well-paid and prestigious appointments are often given for service to the party in power. There are many people who are qualified to serve on the thousands of boards, committees, and agencies that compose part of the state. Why shouldn't members of government appoint the people they know and trust, the people who share their political vision? The problem, at least most of the time, is not evil intent on the part of those in power. The problem is the system itself. In a patronage system, the people appointed owe their jobs to the party in power. It is a rare individual who will then counter the wishes of that party. More important, such appointments are often the pay-off for supporting a political party. With political principle a rarity these days, it is hard to imagine how parties would get workers at all if they couldn't promise jobs and appointments of various kinds to their supporters.

The check on the patronage system is that appointments change each time a new party is elected to government. And in the highest-profile and most important appointments, there are often safeguards in place to ensure that the people appointed are also qualified for the position. Nevertheless, this system does tend to promote the status quo. Unless the party in power has a very strong commitment to equity, the people appointed are likely to reflect the gender, race, and class composition of the government itself.

This bias becomes very clear when we look at the history of the appointment of judges in the province of Ontario. When Ian Scott was the Liberal attorney general in Ontario, from 1985 to 1990, he established a judicial appointments committee. In the past, suggestions for judges were forwarded to the attorney general by the old boys' network of the bar association and by other legal bodies. In his new appointments committee, Scott included lawyers, judges, and most important, a representative group of laypeople. Under

Bob Rae's NDP government, the committee started to advertise for judges, an unheard of break from tradition. Instead of focusing only on lawyers who were highly thought of by their colleagues, thus ensuring a replication of the status quo, the committee began looking for other qualities, including community service and experience with the communities most in conflict with the law. The committee even released an outline of the qualities they were looking for, to which applicants could read and respond. The result was revolutionary. In a few short years, appointments to the bench changed dramatically; many more women and people of colour were included.

My experience with the judicial appointments committee came as a layperson on the Ontario Judicial Council, the body that hears complaints against provincial judges. When I was first appointed to the council, it was still responsible for final approval of the appointment committee's recommendations to the attorney general. Because the committee members spent so much time going over applications and interviewing applicants, the council felt unable to do much more than rubber stamp the appointments, unless there was a glaring error. As a result, the federal court judges who made up the majority of the judicial council were always griping about the process and complaining that it would produce an inferior judiciary. But I believed the opposite was happening. This new process ensured that the people appointed to the bench much more closely resembled the population of the province and were in a much better position to understand the lives of the people coming before them. No one was appointed without the proper legal qualifications, but now it was your community experience and your membership in an under-represented group, not your legal cronies, that put you over the top.

At the time, I believed that the judicial appointments process was one of the most important accomplishments of the Liberal and NDP governments. I still do. But like everything else, the process was overturned by Mike Harris's Tories. The committee still functions, but the attorney general rarely accepts its recommendations.

And since appointments are entirely at the pleasure of the attorney general, there is nothing the committee can do but try to recommend people who will meet with his or her approval. Needless to say, most of the nominees are white males with credentials that please the traditional legal community.

Nevertheless, I don't think judges should be elected, as they are in the U.S., because they should be subject as little as possible to the pressure of elite opinion. The role of a judge is to listen fairly to the facts of a case and the legal arguments, and to judge with neither fear nor favour. I am happy to say that my experience on the judicial council made me much less cynical about how well judges perform this role. Yet however fair and objective judges attempt to be, their life experience colours their judgement. A judiciary that represents only the economic and social elite in society will not always be fair. To ensure that the judiciary represents a more diverse experience than it historically has, we must have a public process for judicial appointments.

Obviously, not every agency, committee, or commission has as its task something as important as the appointment of judges, but in most cases a similar public appointment process could still take place. Governments at all levels could set up appointments committees whose task would be to staff various boards and commissions. It would be composed of both interested and disinterested parties who would be either elected or selected through a process that would ensure regional and demographic representation. The party in power could be allotted a certain number of seats on the appointment committee, and perhaps opposition parties could also be represented, as could the unions acting for civil servants. But the majority of members would be citizens without a link to the party in power. If specific expertise is needed, the appointments committee could hire expert consultants to help evaluate candidates. These bodies could then decide on appointments to boards and agencies based on applicants for the job. The minister responsible could of course also recommend individuals — and these people no doubt would get special consideration from the committee — but the appointments would largely be taken out of the hands of the government of the day.

Participation in government agencies and boards is an excellent path towards active citizenship. People I know who have received appointments to such bodies have, with few exceptions, enjoyed the opportunity to work with others in implementing public policy. As is the case with study groups, the structures are already in place, the resources are already being devoted. All we need to do, in the case of government agencies, boards, and commissions, is set up a democratic system of appointments.

The much bigger question, of course, is how to democratize the public service. Many of the suggestions for public-service reform these days talk about citizens as consumers and government services as commodities. Efficiency replaces public good as the criterion of value. The argument of the right that the market imposes discipline that our current democracy does not is perfectly true. But the provision of public services is only partly the provision of goods and services; it is also the provision of public good, which cannot be measured simply by efficiency and cost. Participatory democracy can set the basis for better accountability in public services through creating citizen watchdog groups and establishing goals and measures that include the public good.

England's Greater London Council (GLC) is probably the most extensive experiment in participatory democracy that we have seen in the developed world in the past few decades. In an article for the book *A Different Kind of State? Popular Power and Democratic Administration*, Robin Murray, who headed up the economic-planning unit of the GLC and later spent time in Canada, says the GLC found that three issues were central to the administration of public services: "How to shift power from officials to elected politicians on the one hand and to users on the other; how to shift the emphasis of regulation in public services from cost accounting to improving services for people; and how to change the internal structure of the state, as well as the relations between manual, clerical and professional workers." The GLC found that trying to strengthen user groups to which individuals subject to abuse can turn for support, legal advice, and advocacy was one way to shift power. Funding campaigns to improve users' awareness of their rights was another.

Democracy Watch is an organization whose goal is to deepen Canadian democracy. Under the leadership of its coordinator, Duff Conacher, Democracy Watch was a central player in the campaign to oppose the bank mergers and has been an important critic of party financing. Democracy Watch has picked up an idea along the lines of the GLC's from Ralph Nader in the United States. The Citizen Utility Board (CUB) is an independent non-profit organization of residential utility ratepayers. Its self-appointed role is to keep watch over the prices of and service offered by utility companies. Nader supporters have managed to organize CUBs in four states in the U.S.; the first one was organized in Wisconsin in 1979. Legislation requires all state utilities to include in their billing once a year a flyer advertising any local CUBs. The flyer informs consumers about the board's activities and invites them to join for a nominal annual membership (ten to fifteen dollars). By piggybacking the flyer with utility bills, CUBs are able to reach many more people than any individual consumer group could ever dream of. The first flyer for the Illinois CUB, for example, was sent out in 1983; within six months, the board had 170,000 members and an annual budget of $1.7 million.

Democracy Watch believes that the CUB model can be used to create citizen associations wherever industry or government is sending public mailings. The organization is currently advocating that the federal government require banks, trust companies, and insurance companies to enclose a one-page flyer advertising a Canadian Financial Consumer Organization (FCO) in their mailings to customers. More than one hundred consumer, small business, student, anti-poverty, labour, and community economic-development groups from across the country have united with

Democracy Watch in the Canadian Community Reinvestment Coalition to advocate for such an organization.

The FCO would be fully democratic. Any individual who pays the annual membership fee would have a vote. Any federal electoral riding with one hundred or more voting members would have the right to elect a delegate from among those members. Once every two years, the delegates would, at the expense of the FCO, attend a national assembly to decide general policy and elect a national board of directors.

Duff Conacher says that if the U.S. experience holds true and there is a 3 percent response rate from the approximately 20 million bank, trust, and insurance customers in Canada, the FCO would have a membership of 600,000 people and, with a membership fee of twenty dollars, annual revenues of $12 million. This would allow it to be completely independent of both government and industry and well enough resourced to take on the big financial institutions when necessary. All that is needed from the government is legislation requiring the financial institutions to include the FCO flyer in their mailings. The Consumer Association, which today is the main advocacy group representing consumers, has, by comparison, 3,000 members and gets grants from banks, insurance companies, and telecommunications companies.

Such citizen-controlled watchdog groups could be set up in any industry, public or private, that does consumer mailings. Democracy Watch is advocating for such groups in the cable-TV, telephone, electricity, gas, airline, and postal industries. They could also be established among users of myriad government services, including unemployment insurance, welfare, pensions, and so on. Here the problem would be what to do with the existing groups that now advocate on behalf of users of these services. My suggestion would be that such groups would form the core of the citizens' associations in those areas. This would give the existing groups a much wider base and greater financial resources, but they would have to be willing to open their organizations to a group of people who might not always agree with their political orientation. In these days of government cuts to advocacy groups, it may be the perfect solution. Instead of wasting precious time and resources in fund-raising activities, these groups could use the CUB idea to create a much cheaper, much broader base of financing.

One of the areas that Democracy Watch has particularly targeted is the health-care system, where, Conacher points out, everyone is organized except the patients. He would like to see a Citizens' Association in Health Care both federally and provincially. "The Canadian Health Care Coalition," he says, "is dominated by the unions. They support a focus on hospitals, which a consumer group might not support." Conacher thinks the unions should be involved in making decisions in the health-care sector, but he doesn't believe that unions and consumers, who sometimes will have diverging interests, should be in the same group. A consumer association in health care would be free to make alliances with the unions on certain issues and act independently on others. While it is true that coalitions between community groups and unions can sometimes be difficult, unions in Canada have been the lifesaver of many advocacy groups. As governments cut funding to the bone, the labour movement has stepped into the breach and provided resources and financing for many groups. The first major national community-union coalition was the Pro-Canada Network, which successfully mobilized a majority of Canadian people to oppose the Free Trade Agreement. The unequal power balance between unions and community groups made this a difficult process, but today, ten years later, unions and community groups have learned to work together more harmoniously. The Days of Action campaign in Ontario, for example, was led by such coalitions, which have had a lasting and positive impact on their communities. I believe that the labour movement in Canada, in conjunction with community groups, has stayed the hand of neo-liberalism longer than in Britain and the U.S. Nevertheless, Conacher's point about the sometimes differing interests of unions and consumers is an important one.

One concern I have with the Democracy Watch idea is that membership could just be on paper. A lot of people might be willing to send ten dollars to a consumer watchdog without wanting to have anything to do with the group after that. A leadership cadre could take over the organization without any real democratic controls, in contrast to most existing advocacy groups, where the membership is active and involved, ensuring a certain level of democratic participation. Nevertheless, citizen associations are an excellent way to organize the users of not only public services but also private services that are essential to the public good. Establishing a consumer advocacy group in an area where there is no existing one, such as the financial-services industry, is an excellent idea. If the prototype citizen association shows that it is an effective advocate for users of the service, the idea may just catch on.

Shifting power to the consumers of public services was one of the strategies of London's GLC. Another was to find ways for elected politicians to spend more of their time on debating public policy and less on the administrative problems of their constituents. In our current system, a lot of the time of individual MPs and their staff is spent on advocating for individual constituents. I realized this most clearly when I became a candidate for political office. Many of the people on whose doors I knocked talked to me about how I could help them personally. They saw me as a person with power, and they were so removed from political power in their own lives that they seized the opportunity to ask for my help or my advice. Friends who have worked in MPPs' offices have told me about spending huge amounts of their time advocating on behalf of citizens with Workers Compensation, the welfare department, and countless other agencies. On the basis of his GLC experience, Robin Murray argues that powerful watchdog organizations would be able to take on much of this work, freeing politicians to spend more time on broader policy issues for their ridings and for their communities as a whole. The politician as individual advocate is part of the patriarchal system of politics; you go to the politician as a supplicant asking for assistance rather than as a citizen proposing solutions.

At the moment, our political system is designed to make us think in terms of our individual problems. If my brother is having a problem with employment insurance and cannot get satisfaction from government workers, for example, he will go to his MP and ask him or her to help him sort out his problem. There is no mechanism for him to find out that others are having the same problem unless he happens to run across an advocacy group in that area. Why shouldn't the government help people with similar problems get together to find creative solutions? If advocacy groups already exist on a given issue, governments should inform their clients.

When it comes to revising the regulatory system, Murray points out that "the word 'bureaucracy' invokes much of what is wrong: red tape, tackling situations by the rulebook rather than with common sense, leaving initiative to the user, engineering situations so that the user rather than the official appears in the wrong, . . . avoiding mistakes instead of solving problems." Indeed, this issue of avoiding mistakes seems to have come to define our entire political process.

"Much depends," continues Murray, "on finding ways of assessing and even measuring the level of services. Since they are not bought and sold, this cannot be done easily in monetary terms. For most services, there are sets of non-cash measures: pupil-teacher rations, miles of streets swept, number of passenger miles travelled on public transit, etc." Service goals should be set democratically and measured so that accountability beyond the bottom line is built into the system. Public servants should be rewarded for initiating improvements in services, rather than simply for error avoidance. Fiscal accountability is, of course, important, but in these neo-liberal times it has become all that seems to matter. It took the nurses' strikes to remind us that public service has to be measured in a great deal more than dollars and cents.

In terms of reorganizing the internal structure of the state, Murray suggests certain immediate steps, including breaking down functional hierarchies and rearranging services around problem-solving groups. "Much of the initiative and creativity in providing services must necessarily come from the state workers, and internal democracy is a necessary condition for such initiative to flourish," he says. This, of course, leads to the need to restructure pay scales and working conditions to reduce the gap among blue-collar, white-collar, and professional workers. Not surprisingly, the Greater London Council ran into major bureaucratic and legal obstacles when it tried to implement such changes. Clearly, we would need a full flowering of a culture of democracy before we could challenge the hierarchical structures of pay and privilege that are present not only in the civil service but also throughout society.

Murray also favours decentralizing functions into service areas. In Canada, this has been tried by a number of provinces, but because it has not been accompanied by an overall democratization, it results only in administrative duplication. The Canadian Hearing Society (CHS), where I worked for almost fifteen years, had to more than double its accounting staff, for example, to keep up with the decentralization of Ontario's Department of Community and Social Services. Decentralization can assist the process of democratization, but the two must go hand in hand.

A lot of the discussion about reforming the administration of the public sector that takes place in official and academic circles these days focuses on what is called the "third sector," or the voluntary sector. In some provinces, there is nothing new in the non-profit sector providing services that in other places are provided by the state. In Ontario, for example, the majority of social services are already provided by third-sector organizations such as the Children's Aid Society. But there is no inherent advantage in third-sector delivery of social services. During the time I worked at CHS, from 1975 to 1990, the agency grew dramatically. Its board members — primarily parents with deaf children and professionals with time on their hands — did not, at first, reflect the people that the organization served. Professional staff members, few of whom were deaf or hard of hearing, ran the agency. But late in the 1980s, when the deaf power movement got stronger, the deaf demanded more representation on the board. While the composition did improve, the board was still controlled by the same elite group that controls almost everything in our society. At the staff level, efforts were made to implement employment equity initiatives, including a management training program for deaf people. The number of deaf and hard-of-hearing staff and management did increase, but the process stagnated during the lean years of the 1990s.

On the other hand, there are numerous grass-roots agencies, such as Foodshare and various co-ops, that have been more democratic in their structure and more creative in their policy initiatives. Social services, in my view, should be delivered by a combination of government-run and publicly funded non-profit agencies. Many of these agencies were developed by citizens who reacted to a need, organized to meet that need, then turned to the government for support. Most women's services began this way, for example. Such creativity in the provision of social services deserves to be supported by public funding, as long as there is accountability. Unfortunately, it is exactly these small grass-roots services that have been so vulnerable to government cuts and to privatization.

One reason why governments are turning to the non-profit sector is that the public generally has more confidence in it. In Ekos Research's *Rethinking Government*, 77 percent of people rated the performance of non-profit, voluntary organizations as good. Only 47 percent rated private companies as good; for government it was 41 percent. Governments also like non-profit organizations because they are usually not unionized; even when they are, the wages are generally lower than in the public sector, which means services can be delivered more cheaply. This does not have to be an argument against third-sector provision of services, but those organizations must be unionized. The Canadian Hearing Society, which is unionized, succeeded in getting increased grants to pay professional salaries equivalent to those for the same jobs in the public sector.

Of course, the major problem with third-sector delivery of social services is that it can be a step to privatization. Needless to say, I believe that there is no place for profit in the provision of social services. The discipline of the market is not what is needed;

it is the desire to meet the needs of the people served that should ensure efficiency. The right likes to argue that the inefficiencies created in the third sector can be solved by privatizing the services and ensuring that the market decides if a service deserves to expand or not. The problem, of course, is that the market works to service those with money. The collapse of affordable housing is an excellent example of how the market fails when it comes to meeting social needs. In fact, housing, more than any other area, shows how disastrous privatization can be. Since the elimination of funding for social housing, there has been no construction at all in this area. In major cities like Toronto, the private sector is not even building affordable rental housing any more.

The most positive reason for offloading services to the third sector is that democratization is much easier to achieve when services are being delivered at the community level. The solution, I believe, is to put in place a combination of government-based and community-based but publicly funded services, and to make these services as decentralized and democratically organized as possible.

8

DEMOCRATIZING THE WELFARE STATE

ONE OF THE BIGGEST THREATS TO DEMOCRACY today is the assault on the welfare state. As a result of this attack, we risk creating a permanent underclass that feels completely disconnected and alienated from society.

Poor-bashing became a national sport in the 1990s, with politicians outdoing each other in their quest to blame welfare recipients for their own poverty. Ontario's Mike Harris went further than most when he cut the pre-natal benefit to pregnant women on welfare and said it was so they wouldn't spend the money on beer. Prime Minister Jean Chrétien has also equated welfare recipients with drunks. "In my judgement," he told a black-tie audience in 1994, "it is better to have them at 50 percent productivity than sitting at home, drinking beer, at zero percent productivity." Even NDP premiers have joined in the poor-bashing. Former B.C. premier Mike Harcourt, in announcing welfare reforms, said, "We want to clean the cheats and deadbeats off the welfare rolls. . . . We're not going to allow people who could and should be in the workforce to sit there and do nothing."

What's the reality of people on welfare? The highest level of welfare fraud I have ever seen quoted is 4 percent, and it is usually less than 2 percent. There is more fraud going on in the Skydome on any given Saturday, when businessmen take their families to tax-deductible boxes that are supposed to be for business associates, than takes place in every welfare office across the country put together. Yet we spend millions on policing the poor.

The National Council of Welfare's *Welfare Myths and Realities* exposes a lot of the welfare myths. Contrary to the popular belief that most welfare recipients are lazy, good-for-nothing young people looking for a free ride, for example, the report points out that only 4 percent of welfare cases were under the age of twenty and only another 12 percent were between twenty and twenty-five. Another powerful myth is that teenage women get pregnant to get welfare. The reality is that only 3 percent of single parents on welfare were under age twenty; nearly half of all single-parent families on welfare had only one child, and another 31 percent had only two children.

Of course, the facts rarely get in the way of scapegoating. Nevertheless, the recent crisis of homelessness has somewhat countered the impulse towards poor-bashing. It seems that if people are on the street and hungry, we can afford to give them some sympathy, but if they are getting enough to pay rent and buy food, we just want them to get a job and work hard like the rest of us.

In 1988, a brief moment of sanity regarding the development of the welfare state emerged in Ontario. A report called *Transitions* proposed a series of reforms that were supported by poor people and Conrad Black alike. This was the fundamental objective that was to guide these reforms:

> All people in Ontario are entitled to an equal assurance of life opportunities in a society that is based on fairness, shared responsibility and personal dignity for all. The objective of social assistance therefore must be to ensure that individuals are able to make the transition from dependence to autonomy and from exclusion on the margins of society to integration within the mainstream of community life.

Instead of targeting the poor for blame, the report looked at what elements of the social-assistance network undermined independence. It then laid out several principles that were to direct the provision of social services, including the fundamental principle that poor people had a right to "a fair and equitable level of social assistance adequate to meet their basic needs." Some of the other principles of the report were outlined thus: "The social assistance system must enable individuals to assume responsibility for themselves and must ensure choice, self-determination and participation in community life. [It] must respect the rights of individuals guaranteed in the Canadian Charter of Rights and Freedoms and other laws. It must guarantee a clear and impartial decision-making process. . . . The administration of social assistance must be efficient, open and publicly accountable."

The *Transitions* report was the result of extensive consultation with poor people, workers in the poverty industry, and the community at large. It had massive and widespread support, and it provided a blueprint for progressive reform of the welfare system. It was probably the last gasp of the liberal welfare state — and remains one of its finer moments. Today, it sits in the dustbin of history while Mike Harris piles assault after assault on poor people with barely a murmur of public opposition.

We have regressed to Victorian notions of the deserving and undeserving poor. We talk about child poverty as if the parents didn't exist. We are willing to provide benefits to the working poor, but only at the expense of the poor on welfare. Social assistance is even disappearing as a public issue. Politicians of every ideological stripe are competing to be seen as the saviours of medicare and education, the concerns of the middle class. As a result, the people hurt most by the zeal of deficit reduction also benefit least from "re-investment."

The dangers of this attack on the poor are best seen from the United States, where it started almost thirty years ago. In her article "Reforming the Welfare State," in the book *A Different Kind of State*, Frances Fox Piven, a professor at City University of New York, points out that the high poverty levels in the United States also explain "other unique features of the American labour market in the 1980s, including the collapse of unionism, falling wage levels, lengthening work hours, explosive growth in low-wage and irregular jobs, and widening income polarization. In short, history was providing a virtual laboratory for the examination of the significance of welfare-state related programs for class inequalities and class power relations."

Criminalization of the poor went hand in hand with cuts to social assistance in the U.S. No one is in prison simply for being poor, of course, but without income or access to decent jobs, more and more young people will try to escape through drugs or profit through crime. In fact, the United States has already imprisoned a significant percentage of its poor male population. In the past fifteen years, the prison population there has tripled. With its 1997 rate of 645 people imprisoned for every 100,000 in the population, the U.S. was incarcerating a higher percentage of its population than South Africa did under apartheid. When you count the number of people on parole and probation, 5.4 million Americans were in the prison system. That is 5 percent of the total male population and 20 percent of the black male population. Some analysts have estimated that unemployment rates in the U.S. would be 2 percentage points higher if they included all the men in prison.

The American writer Barbara Ehrenreich, speaking at a November 1998 conference on democracy and equality that was sponsored by Simon Fraser University and broadcast by CBC Radio's "Ideas" program, pointed to the danger to democracy of this type of punitive-minded philosophy. "When government spends little or nothing on social assistance," she said, "and more and more on the repressive forces of the state — police, prisons, and military — poor people begin to see government as the problem rather than a solution. All a ghetto-dwelling black male sees of the government is police and prison guards. The idea that electing a politician could promote community interests becomes more and more remote." That is one explanation for why the majority of Americans feel alienated from their electoral system.

Mike Harris in Ontario has certainly learned from the American laboratory. Savage 22 percent cuts to welfare rates were one of the first actions of his government when the Tories were elected in 1995. A mother of two now receives only $1,239 a month. That means, after rent is paid, struggling to survive on $5.91 a day for each person in the family. Statistics from the Daily Bread Food Bank in Toronto reveal that 16 percent of mothers reported that their children go without food at least once a week. In another study, 80 percent of mothers reported cutting down on their own meals and 20 percent going without eating for an entire day. More than half had to give up telephone or other services in order to have money for food. Since the cuts, the use of food banks across the province has skyrocketed.

After his second electoral victory, in 1999, Harris began to move to the next stage of his war on the poor. Despite the fact that violent crime rates are going down in Ontario, as elsewhere, Harris's election platform included a priority focus on "safety." He particularly targeted squeegee kids and "harassment" by aggressive panhandlers. Cut welfare and social housing to throw poor people into the streets and then arrest them for trying to eke out a living — fiscally, this makes no sense at all. Putting someone in prison or even in a hostel is more expensive than providing a decent income and placing a modest roof over his head. The assault on the poor is purely political.

Progressive organizations have spent most of the past fifteen years arguing against cuts to social assistance and unemployment insurance, not to mention health and education programs. But now, in the face of these savage attacks from the right, such groups have found themselves in the odd position of defending the existing welfare state. And yet, feminists have certainly never supported the bureaucratic welfare state as it currently exists. The system of welfare delivery has always been patriarchal, patronizing, and demeaning to women. Nevertheless, when confronted with an ideological assault on the very idea of welfare, in addition to a financial and increasingly repressive assault on low-income people themselves, defending the status quo seems like the best option.

The problem is not that the state cannot afford welfare. The problem is that the right has persuaded people that the poor and unemployed are responsible for their own situations, and that what they need is not support but a kick in the butt. Yet even though support for passive income assistance (i.e., welfare) has declined, the general public is still much more compassionate towards the poor than the elites are. In Ekos' *Rethinking Government 1998*, 61 percent of people agreed that the inadequate income of poor families was a result of low social-assistance levels; only 40 percent of decision-makers agreed with this statement. Most decision-makers believed that inferior values and family practices among poor families produced poverty; only 28 percent of the general public felt this way.

Meanwhile, support for activist government also remains high. Fully 64 percent of the general public agreed that Canada's social programs have a major impact on our overall quality of life. Still, 66 percent also agreed that traditional social programs such as social assistance and EI have encouraged dependency on public assistance; that figure goes up to 76 percent for decision-makers. But 60 percent said that too many people have been hurt by the cuts to social programs, and that now it's time to strengthen our commitment to the social safety net.

At heart, welfare and unemployment cuts reflect the unwillingness of the economic and political elites to share their wealth through state redistribution. The current focus of the right on tax cuts, despite very little initial public support for this issue, demonstrates my point. If what was really driving welfare cuts was the fiscal crisis of the state, then today we should be seeing an enormous injection of cash back into this and other social programs. Instead, the mean-spirited and punitive direction of workfare is proceeding; except for the child tax benefit, which in most provinces supplements the income of the working poor, there has been no move to improve the dismal social-assistance rates.

Instead of direct income support based on simple need, the welfare state developed a complex bureaucracy to police recipients on the one hand and to assist them on another. The complexity of funding welfare through federal-provincial cost-shared programs makes it difficult to judge how much of the money designated for welfare goes directly into the pockets of the poor and how much goes into funding the massive state bureaucracy and web of private non-profit agencies that anti-poverty groups call the poverty industry. For my purposes, I am most interested in the way in which the poverty industry helped foster dependence and passivity among the poor.

In her 1998 book *No Car, No Radio, No Liquor Permit: The Moral Regulation of Single Mothers in Ontario, 1920–1997*, the political scientist Margaret Little documents the patronizing, demeaning, and often humiliating policies that have long been imposed on single mothers receiving welfare payments. After making an exhaustive study of Ontario's mothers' allowance, Little interviewed single mothers on welfare today and concluded: "Current single mothers on welfare encounter both financial and moral regulation of their lives. Although the definition of worthiness has changed over time, perhaps what is most remarkable is the fact that social workers continue to expend considerable energy in this determination."

Such treatment undermines the very confidence and sense of self-worth of many welfare recipients. As a result, this oppression of the welfare system does produce a certain passivity among its recipients. If everyone from the premier to your own social worker is giving you the message that you are shiftless and worthless, it is not surprising that you are not motivated to sell yourself in the marketplace. Sadly, what Little calls "the moral regulation of single mothers" can be applied in general to our attitude towards the poor in the age of neo-liberalism.

Yet providing social assistance for those who fall on hard times is a vital element of a civilized society. Although Canada's welfare state is far from the most generous, it did do a good job of countering the massive gap in income produced by market forces in the 1960s, 1970s, and 1980s. In her *Growing Gap* report, published by the Centre for Social Justice in 1998, the economist Armine Yalnizyan showed that if poor people had to rely on market income alone, they would be totally destitute. The average earnings of the poorest 10 percent of families fell from $7,220 in 1973 (in 1996 dollars) to $1,823 in 1996. In 1973, almost two-thirds of low-income families had some work. Today, almost three-quarters do not.

Up until 1990, when we began to see the major cuts to unemployment insurance and social assistance, the gap between rich and poor remained fairly constant. This stability reflected the salutary impact of government assistance on those temporarily or permanently out of work. But since the massive cuts to income support, that gap has expanded exponentially. Yalnizyan showed that in 1973, rich families earned 18 times more than poor families; by 1996 they were earning 314 times more. Much of that dramatic change has taken place in the past few years, further evidence of the effects of government cutbacks and economic restructuring.

In the meantime, the nature of work itself has changed, and the restructuring of the workforce to create more marginal jobs and more self-employment is expanding the ranks of the working poor. These changes, when combined with the cuts to welfare and EI, are seriously undermining many of the gains that workers in Canada have made over the past two generations. In the 1990s, the before-tax real income of Canadians declined by $425. If we look at just private market income, excluding government transfers, we find that each Canadian actually lost $772. During the same period, tax increases accounted for only $410 per capita. In other words, most of the drop in living standards that we are experiencing is caused by declining wages, not increasing taxes.

Unemployment levels remain unacceptably high. There are still 3.2 million Canadians who are unemployed or significantly underemployed. That is one-fifth of the workforce. The official unemployment rate was 8.4 percent in May 1999, but that rate reflects only those actively searching for work. The structural exclusion rate includes those who have stopped looking for work or those who are significantly underemployed, and it was 20.3 percent for the same month.

But nothing is threatening the middle class more than the shift from full-time jobs to non-standard work. A study done by Mike Burke and John Shields of Ryerson Polytechnic University found that 45 percent of adult employees between the ages of twenty-five and forty-nine are employed in flexible forms of work (this includes part-time, contract, and full-time non-permanent work). On average, this non-standard work pays five to eight dollars an hour less than full-time work. This type of work is also totally insecure and provides little opportunity for job advancement.

Self-employment accounted for 60 percent of new jobs created in the past decade in Canada. According to Armine Yalnizyan, more than 16 percent of those working for themselves in 1995 made less than $5,000 a year; only 3 percent of paid employees fell into that category. Only at the very top of the income scale are self-employed people doing better than waged workers. Self-employed women earn about half of what men do; in the waged workforce it's closer to 73 percent. In addition to earning less, self-employed people have no benefits, no unemployment insurance, and no job security. Self-employment has positive elements as well, of course, including more flexibility and personal freedom. I myself am self-employed and prefer it to a steady job, but for me it was a choice rather than a necessity.

The insecurity of non-standard work has a negative impact on democracy in a number of ways. First, people spend all their time and energy just providing for their families. In that Ekos survey I referred to earlier, fully 42 percent of respondents agreed with the statement "These days I'm so hard-pressed to take care of my own needs that I worry less about the needs of others." Insecurity undermines the bonds of social solidarity, and job insecurity seriously weakens workers in their relationships with their bosses. This has led to the successful undermining of labour rights in many advanced capitalist countries. The Canadian labour movement has weathered these attacks better than most, but in the right-wing provinces there has been a serious decline in labour standards. Ontario's Bill 7, for example, made it much more difficult to organize by eliminating automatic certification, no matter how many union cards are signed.

The attacks on the welfare state are an attack on democracy. They violate and undermine the social contract that provided a share of wealth and security to working people after the Second World War. Meanwhile, rapid changes in the global economy caused by the collapse of communism, technological advances, and the triumph of neo-liberalism in the English-speaking capitalist world have changed the balance of power massively in favour of the economic elites. Yet instead of responding to this economic restructuring with stronger social programs to protect the unemployed and those in marginal employment, the federal government has done the opposite. In 1989, 70 percent of unemployed Canadians were eligible for unemployment insurance benefits; by 1997 only 34 percent were covered. Young people and women were the hardest hit. According to a 1999 report from Human Resources Canada, women's EI claims dropped by 20 percent while men's claims dropped 16 percent. Claims for those under age twenty-five dropped by 27 percent, while claims for those forty-five to fifty-four dropped by only 8 percent. The lower figures for youth and women reflect the increased difficulty part-time workers have qualifying for employment insurance.

In a society where the welfare of its citizens was once paramount, those most hurt by private-sector restructuring should be the focus of reform. But Finance Minister Paul Martin's EI reforms make the poor pay. Martin sold his changes by claiming that part-time workers would be covered because eligibility would be judged by hours of work, rather than weeks of work. The reality is that thousands of part-time workers now pay into the fund without much hope of ever collecting insurance when they are laid off or become pregnant. With fewer and fewer workers eligible for employment insurance, the public is more and more easily persuaded by the corporate media that the system is not worth saving. This is how the neo-liberal assault on social programs works.

Instead of simply defending the existing welfare state with the moral argument that ours is a caring, sharing society, progressive people should be developing a more democratic, more activist, and more egalitarian model of welfare. I'll now turn to what I believe should be some of the elements of such a model.

More and more in recent years, anti-poverty groups are turning towards the United Nations and the idea of a rights-based approach to ending poverty. As mentioned earlier, the UN International Covenant on Economic, Social and Cultural Rights, which Canada has signed, ensures that all people have the right to food and shelter. Anti-poverty groups have been fighting for the courts to enshrine these rights in our Charter of Rights and Freedoms. While I agree that poor people should be included in the equality section of the charter, I don't think this will solve the problem of poverty. Nevertheless, a legal right to a decent income would go a long way to reducing the oppression of these low-income people, and there is a possibility that anti-poverty groups will succeed in convincing the Supreme Court to read "income level" into the charter, as has been done for sexual orientation. If this happens, it will create a whole new momentum in the fight for the rights of poor people. But there are deeper issues that require examination.

Jean Swanson, former president of the National Anti-Poverty Organization and currently a member of End Legislated Poverty in Vancouver, says poor-bashing goes beyond the crass comments of politicians and media pundits. It is pervasive in our attitudes towards the poor. "Even the questions we ask about the poor show our prejudice," she says. "We ask, 'How can we help the poor? How can we get people off welfare and onto work?' What we should be asking is, 'How can we reduce poverty? How can we get the rich to share? How can we get jobs with adequate income?'"

In 1998, Peter Munk, the CEO of Barrick Gold, took home $38,918,951 in compensation. Richard Currie of Loblaws got $34,122,152. This was a 1,283 percent increase for Munk and a 343 percent increase for Currie. Poor Frank Stronach of Magna had a 16.1 percent decrease, leaving him in third place with only

$26,154,250. Three other CEOs made more than $10 million each and ten others made more than $5 million. Such massive salaries are justified by the argument that it is the only way to attract the best talent to run Canadian corporations. Swanson has often asked why it is that society believes that we have to pay mega-bucks to corporate leaders to get them to work, but the way to get the poor to work is to starve and humiliate them. Often when discussing these issues on radio talk shows, I am told that higher taxes will discourage people from working harder and producing more. The assumption is that the only motivating factor for work and creativity is money. Yet when it comes to poor people, the expectation is that they will be motivated by a withdrawal of money. It is almost as if some people feel that low-income earners are a different breed than the rest of us. Someone once said that you can judge a society by how it treats its most vulnerable citizens. By that standard, Canada is rapidly becoming a dismal failure. An alternative vision of society has to include a realistic project of economic democratization. Extreme social inequality creates an underclass, and that underclass feels excluded from political and social life.

For democracy to function there must be some level of economic equality. Closing the income gap is an essential step to active citizenship and deepening democracy. The minimum wage has been declining in value for the past fifteen years. Raising it would increase the potential for all low-income jobs. Giving workers in non-standard positions (i.e., temporary or part-time jobs) the same benefits as full-time workers is another urgent priority. Changing labour law to permit easier organizing for unions would, in turn, significantly improve wages and working conditions for those members of the workforce who are today not unionized. And most important, economic policy has to be designed to stimulate job creation everywhere, including in the public sector. Our goal must be to eliminate poverty, not to make poor people disappear from public space.

In Canada, social assistance is the responsibility of the provinces. Nevertheless, through the defunct Canada Assistance Plan (CAP), UI, pensions, and now the child tax benefit, the federal government has played a major role in the operation of the welfare state. Indeed, the rapid decline of social assistance since the elimination of CAP provides an illustration of the importance of national standards. It is essential that the federal government retain its role.

Although the issue of decentralization emerges internationally in discussions of the welfare state, we obviously have a special situation in Canada. Social activists in Quebec look to the province, not the federal government, to guarantee their rights, whether economic or political. In fact, many Québécois cannot understand why activists in English Canada insist on defending the role of the federal state. And indeed it can probably be said that our focus on the federal state has been something of an obsession over the past fifteen years. In 1991, the National Action Committee on the Status of Women developed support for the idea of a three nations model, with Quebec and the aboriginal nations being given the right and the resources to develop social programs that are autonomous from the federal state. Unfortunately, since no elected politician has ever been willing to make the argument for what they call asymmetrical federalism, this idea has never taken hold in English Canada. But the new social union agreement may provide a framework for this kind of approach.

Still, the best model, I believe, is for the federal government to provide direct income support and fund services based on standards for the provision of those services. Then the provincial governments can organize the delivery of services in co-operation with community organizations. While private non-profit organizations have an essential role to play, public funding and public accountability are essential.

There is an even stronger argument for state provision of social assistance. The redistribution of wealth through the tax system and through social programs has long been a hallmark of the welfare state. While reforms are an essential response to the challenges of the new century, the ideas that government should help provide a decent way of life for all of its citizens and that in a civilized society the rich should pay more of their share for the provision of services are central to any kind of just or equal society.

Thirty years ago, progressive groups working with the poor proposed the idea of a guaranteed annual income as a way of eliminating poverty. The idea was that the government would deliver a cheque to all Canadians who had income below a certain level. Everyone who needed it would have their income topped up to a liveable wage. No judgement would be made on why an individual needed the top-up; it would simply be based on financial need. The system would be policed in the same way as the tax system — that is, to ensure that people were correctly reporting their income. Services for job training, language training, addiction treatment, mental health counselling, or anything else would be accessible to everyone. The assumption was that people would get work if they were able and, if for whatever reason they were not able or if their job paid below a certain minimum, they would have the right to government assistance. This idea is a long way from public consciousness today, but it warrants examination.

In 1985, when the Macdonald Commission put forward the idea of a guaranteed annual income, the left gave it up. The commission, which was looking into Canada's economic union and development prospects, proposed a guaranteed annual income as a recognition of the consistently high levels of unemployment. The idea was that people would be paid the equivalent of welfare rates if they couldn't find work. This way, the government, rather than devoting all its resources to job creation, would ensure a survival-level income for all citizens. Progressive critics correctly pointed out that such a policy would condemn marginalized people to inhabit the margins of society forever. More recent proposals for a guaranteed annual income — or basic income, as it has come to be called — have been linked to ideas of the end of work. But it is not necessary to believe that paid work can no longer provide adequate income to the majority in order to support the idea of basic income

(BI). There is no reason why BI could not be combined with vig-orous job-creation, education, childcare, and training policies. Of course, any BI program would have to be combined with the right to paid employment, to ensure that no one would be forced to sub-sist only on BI.

At the moment, we have a confusing array of geared-to-income support programs, from the child tax benefit to employment insur-ance to old-age pensions. There are enormous bureaucracies supporting and delivering all these systems, and embedded within them are certain moral judgements. Children are blameless and should not suffer for the sins (such as being underemployed) of their parents. Old people deserve state support because they con-tributed. Income support for poor people will encourage them to be lazy and shiftless. Getting employment insurance is less of a stigma than getting welfare because it only means you are between jobs.

Our different income-support programs are based on these moral judgements. With no questions asked, seniors get govern-ment pensions based on their income or the contributions they made. People on employment insurance have to show that they are looking for work, but otherwise can get paid without being asked intrusive and humiliating questions by government workers. People on welfare, on the other hand, face degrading and humiliating inter-ference in their lives. The child benefit cheque is an improvement, because it is based on income and is delivered through the tax system without an expensive policing mechanism. Unfortunately, provincial governments can tax back this amount from people on social assistance, so it is not helping the poorest of the poor. And thus it becomes yet another example of how income support is delivered in a punitive way to the poor.

If we begin from the moral position that no one in society should fall below a certain standard of living, then there is no reason why all these programs could not be combined into a single geared-to-income support program. So many people would benefit from such a program over their lifetimes that it would be able to maintain considerably more public support than welfare currently does. It would also mean a tremendous simplification in the delivery of services. It would provide income security for everyone, no matter how insecure their employment or family situation. It would permit the separation of service delivery from income support, and thus perhaps simplify federal-provincial issues, with the federal government taking responsibility for income support and the provinces for service delivery, although with national standards.

BI could provide the basis for revaluing paid and unpaid work. At one time, wages were high enough for a man to support his entire family. Employers paid a generous wage that, on the surface, remunerated only the worker himself, but in reality also paid for the work of his wife in caring for him and their children. The family wage is long gone, however, and most couples today need two incomes to support themselves. As a result, unpaid work in the home and community is becoming more and more of a burden on women.

I believe that the best solution to this problem is twofold: government funding for a universal childcare program and men assuming a larger share of child-rearing activities. But I also understand the desire of some parents to spend more time with their children. I think that parents should have a real choice, and that they should be supported in that choice.

The proposal for BI provides more freedom for people to choose how central paid work is to their lifestyle. A family could decide for one parent to stay home with their children, for example, or for both to work full time. This would apply equally to single parents. There would still be an income differential between those who are in the waged workforce and those who are not, but individuals could decide for themselves whether they preferred the time with their family or the additional money. At the moment, only families with considerably higher than average income can afford to make such choices. Current proposals for tax cuts to families with stay-at-home parents favour high-income earners and create a state policy of pushing women back into the home.

A BI would also permit realistic lifelong learning options. A person could take a year or two off every once in a while to study, for example. The CAW negotiates such educational time for its members, so why shouldn't everyone in society have access to such benefits? And a BI would allow people more time to participate in civic life. The proposals for direct democracy outlined throughout this book require that citizens receive time and compensation for their participation in the democratic life of our country. A BI would ensure that every citizen who chooses to could take the time to fully participate in exciting new ways to share political power.

There are numerous proposals for how such an income-support program could be paid for. Certainly simplifying the current income-support system would free up considerable sums of money. Imposing new taxes on the financial sector, which has profited enormously from the restructured economy, could also finance such a scheme. Perhaps the program could also be structured partly as an insurance scheme, so that every worker and every employer would contribute to the BI through premiums, as we do now with unemployment insurance and the Canada Pension Plan but with the difference that benefits would be universally available.

Unfortunately, the idea of instituting a guaranteed annual income at a liveable level is clearly far from the realities of today's politics. At the moment, we must fight for the restoration of social-assistance rates, insist that child benefits go to social assistance recipients without penalty, and remove the punitive aspects of "welfare reform." But a long-term vision is necessary to counter the "us and them" attitude promoted by the right.

There should be no specific social programs targeted at the poor and unemployed. All training and support programs should be available to everyone. Targeted programs simply reinforce the existing stigma against the poor, and we have learned over the past fifteen years that only universal social programs can attract the public support necessary to withstand periodic attacks from the economic elites. All training programs, from basic literacy and life skills to advanced technical training, should be available to everyone who needs them.

Similarly, mental health and addiction programs should be universally available. Classism is perhaps most visible in our society's treatment of the poor and the mentally ill, and nowhere is the danger of privatizing public services clearer than in these areas. People with money to pay for private psychologists or addiction programs are much more likely to live productive lives than those without that opportunity.

And of course, any new model for the welfare state has to include support for families with children. Indeed, the feminization of poverty is the clearest indication of the failure of the current welfare state to support families. A more generous maternity and parental-leave program would permit parents to stay home with their children, should they choose, for one year. Publicly funded childcare would ensure that poor children do not start life with the odds stacked against them.

In Quebec in 1997, the Parti Québécois government began funding a program of regulated childcare for all four-year-olds. Parents pay only five dollars a day. In September 1998, the program was extended to include three-year-olds; the following year, two-year-olds were added and finally so will one-year-olds. By the end of the roll-out, available childcare spaces will more than double. Parents can choose which kind of childcare they prefer, either centre-based (i.e., the traditional day-care centre) or family-based (i.e., private, non-profit, in-home care). But to participate in the five-dollar-a-day plan, the childcare must be regulated.

The five-dollar-a-day program has been so popular that parents have moved their children into regulated care at great speed. When rumours started circulating that implementation of the program for three-year-olds would be slowed down because of budget constraints, there was enough of a public outcry to ensure that the popular program would remain intact. In the 1999 provincial election campaign, even the Liberals supported the program because it was so popular. And therein lies a good lesson about the importance of universality to social programs. If childcare had been provided only to poor children, it is unlikely that the public uproar

would have been sufficient enough to pressure a government struggling with its deficit to continue the policy.

Children in Canada are treated like consumer items, the private
responsibility of parents. But at the same time, the ambiguity about
women's roles in the workplace has resulted in a paralysis of social
policy that means Canadians have neither universal childcare nor a
tax credit/family allowance to offset the cost of raising children.
Canada needs to develop a series of social and fiscal policies that
recognize the value society places on children, as well as the additional cost to families of raising children. Fortunately, some recent
studies on the importance of early childhood education, combined
with the success of Quebec's five-dollar-a-day program, is starting
to put the issue of childcare back on the agenda.

And there are other social programs that could easily be applied
universally. Even food support programs can be universal. A good
example is the Field to Table program, a division of Foodshare
in Toronto. This is a grass-roots program that provides subscribers
with a box of fresh "good food" every week for fifteen dollars. Food
is distributed to volunteers in various neighbourhoods, and poor
and middle-class people enjoy the same benefits for the same price.
As well as providing more fresh food than most poor people would
normally eat, the so-called Good Food Box includes simple nutrition information and recipes. It also offers a community connection
that most people in urban centres no longer have.

So how does the program work? The basket is available for free
or at a reduced price for poor people, who in exchange work in the
distributing centre. They are asked to work only as much as they
are able to. Because Foodshare deals directly with farmers, the price
is kept low for everyone. As a result, poorer people, instead of going
to a food bank and getting charity, are able to purchase fresh food
like everyone else.

According to Foodshare's director, Debbie Field, the crisis of
the welfare state is a result, in part, of the creation of a passive con-

sumer model for the delivery of welfare. In reality, poor people want to contribute and give back like everyone else. At Field to Table, they are included and made part of the process. According to Field, this co-operative, democratic approach, as opposed to the punitive nature of workfare, is successful because it considers working to be part of the way that poor people pay for the services they get.

Community agencies like Field to Table are developing all kinds of innovative ways to democratize the welfare state. While the agencies themselves are private, in the sense that they are community controlled, their funding is public and so is their accountability.

Still, whether services are provided directly by government or through non-profit agencies, the key is the democratic participation of both stakeholders and citizens. Any reorganization of the delivery of services or income support has to include poor people in its design, as was suggested by the *Transitions* report in Ontario. Even adding an advisory board of low-income people to existing programs would be an improvement. Instead of groups like the National Council of Welfare and the National Anti-Poverty Organization being voices in the wilderness, they should be central to any redesign of social assistance. With the government opting out of offering any real assistance to the poor, community groups have taken over. From the Downtown East Side Residents' Association in Vancouver to St. Christopher's House in Toronto, community groups are providing on-the-street assistance to poor people in every city across the country. It is to these groups and their clients that governments should turn to develop a more humane, more responsive, and ultimately more successful system of social support. Democratizing the welfare state means not only redistributing income so that working people have the security to participate more fully in the democratic process, in their communities, and in their families, but also restructuring service delivery to significantly include that participation.

9

YOUR TIME OR YOUR MONEY

FOR MOST OF MY LIFE, MONEY didn't mean a lot to me. Like most people in my generation of middle-class North Americans, I never had to worry much about a job. If I took time off work to travel or study, as I did in the early 1970s, there would always be a job available for me later. During the 1980s, I worked at a professional-level job at the Canadian Hearing Society. I made a comfortable living, lived in a one-bedroom apartment in a decidedly unfashionable part of Toronto, and had enough money to take a holiday every year. That was all I wanted. My passion was political activism. As long as my job gave me the flexibility to be able to organize politically, I was satisfied.

When I became president of NAC, it was the first time I had ever been paid to do the political work I love. Then, for a year after I stepped down in 1993, I did contract work. The money was good, but I hated the isolation of working alone most of the time. After a nine-month stint as a visiting professor at the University of Regina, I got a phone call asking if I would be interested in being the left-wing host of a debate show on CBC Newsworld. The call had come from out of the blue. In fact, I had already accepted a job as Canadian director of CUSO, an international development agency, and was in the midst of plans to move to Ottawa. But I had been nervous about going into a totally new area of work, and about moving to a new city. Co-hosting this debate show, which came to be called "Face Off," seemed like the perfect fit for me, so I accepted. Many things changed for me after starting work at "Face Off," but I want to talk here about the impact of almost doubling my income.

By TV standards, my host job was not that well paid. But $85,000 a year was 50 percent more than I had been making at either NAC or CHS. On top of that, I was still doing other media commentary and some writing, which brought my income to almost $100,000 a year. Suddenly my latent consumerist tendencies blossomed. I felt like I had more money than I knew what to do with. My spending soon accelerated way beyond my income.

The first thing I learned about television is that you have to buy clothes. I used to hate shopping, because my domineering father loved it and always wanted to take me along. But with my new position, I easily overcame both that aversion and my feminist hesitations on spending too much energy on my appearance. Indeed, I had learned over the years as a spokesperson that looking good on television has a major impact on whether people listen to you. If how you look becomes an issue, no one will listen to what you say. Faced with this knowledge, I soon found that I got into the joy of shopping in a big way.

To be fair to myself, my sixteen-year-old nephew moved in with me at around this same time, and having a teenage dependent costs a lot of money. I moved into a two-bedroom apartment so there would be room for Lucas. And then, of course, I had to furnish the apartment, so I went shopping for furniture. At first, I just bought the practical things: an office unit because I had no separate work space; a wardrobe for the front hall; a kitchen table and chairs because my old table didn't fit in the new house. I just put the stuff on a credit card, knowing that I was making enough money to easily pay it off. Well, to make a long story short, I soon found myself $30,000 in debt on credit cards alone. I wasn't living in the lap of luxury by any means, but I was tricked by the attitude that I could buy anything I wanted now because I had a higher income. I was lucky that my spending spree took place after the years of high interest rates were over, or I would really have got into trouble. To this day, I find that the only way I can avoid spending money is to stay out of the stores.

When I look at the spending habits of North Americans, I know that my behaviour is not unusual. In Canada, in the final quarter of 1998, the average personal debt was greater than the average disposable income for the first time since Statistics Canada began collecting these figures in the early 1960s. For most people, the problem stems from a combination of consumerism, credit card availability, and stagnant real incomes.

Consumerism is an incredible trap. The illusion of our consumer society is that the more things you have, the happier you will be. When I was growing up, it was called keeping up with the Joneses. My parents and others of their generation wanted everything their neighbours had. Men got their value by being good providers, and the proof was the house in the suburbs, the two cars in the garage, the TV and then the colour TV, the modern appliances, and so on.

My generation rebelled against the materialism of our parents. Hippies threw off the desires of affluent society and opted for voluntary poverty, which of course, because it was chosen, was nothing like real poverty. I remember organizing a tent city for transient youth in the summer of 1971. This project was funded by an Opportunities for Youth (OFY) grant, one of the various federal grants available for young people at the time. It is hard to believe today, but during our negotiations with the federal bureaucrat in charge we actually asked for less money for salaries than he was offering.

I rejected the material basis of my parents' happiness. To me, it seemed that all they really cared about was money and success. I believed that I, and politicized young people like me, had higher ideals. Unfortunately most of us, even those who continued to be politically active long after their teens and early twenties, left the critique of consumerism behind. While few of the radicals of my youth have joined the ranks of the rich and famous, most of us have adopted the middle-class lifestyles set out for us by the advertising industry. Only the environmental movement has maintained the critique of consumerism, and even then the focus has been much more on saving endangered species and forests than on challenging the consumer habits of the North.

Is it any wonder that our children, who for the most part have much less opportunity than we did, have bought into consumerism hook, line, and sinker? Keeping up with the Joneses has been transformed into a necessity to have whatever is hip, cool, or in style in any given season. From the must-have toys of children to the logo clothes of teens to the fashion and cosmetic trends of twentysomethings, the latest generation is more plugged into consumerism than our parents ever were.

The neo-cons want to convince us that through consumerism we have power. The first time I heard this argument was during a meeting with the *Globe and Mail* editorial board in 1993 to discuss the North American Free Trade Agreement (NAFTA). Andrew Coyne, at the time one of the new hotshot editorialists at the *Globe*, claimed that free trade gave people new power, the power of consumers. Political institutions were bureaucratized and not responsive to citizens, he argued. Markets, on the other hand, had to be responsive to consumers. As more and more services were privatized, he reasoned, we would have more control through what we purchased. This would ensure higher-quality and more responsive services through competition.

At first I thought he was kidding. But time and time again since then, I have heard this argument from free marketeers. In a truly democratic society, people would laugh at such an argument. If one person, one vote is the essence of electoral democracy, then surely the extension of electoral democracy must be based on the same egalitarian ideal. Basing democracy on consumerism means giving the most power to those with the most money. In our society, those with the most money already have the most power. Democratization surely has to be about countering, not reinforcing, this power.

Yet the strange twist on political debate at the turn of the twenty-first century is that the charlatans of neo-liberalism have managed to convince us that reinforcing privilege is the best way to achieve prosperity for all. "What's good for General Motors is good for the U.S.A." This slogan, summing up the heyday of American capitalism, has been developed into economic and political theory by the economic elites. Meanwhile, the neo-conservatives who have taken over our governments are trying to convince us that a tax cut that puts an average of $500 a year extra in our pockets is more important than protecting a universal education system or ensuring that no one in our society is homeless or hungry.

It is not that we have become heartless, selfish people. It is, on the one hand, that we are struggling to maintain the lifestyle to which we have become accustomed and, on the other hand, that we no longer trust governments to provide the collective services that we would like to see. Huge industries are devoted to convincing us that private spending will make us happy, secure, beautiful, sexy, and healthy. The reality, however, is that most of us can afford less now than our parents and grandparents could.

In her *Growing Gap* report, the economist Armine Yalnizyan points out that in 1973, the top 10 percent of families earned an average income 21 times higher than that earned by those at the bottom ($107,000 compared with $5,200, in 1996 dollars). By 1996, the top 10 percent earned 314 times as much as families at the bottom ($137,000 compared with less than $500). She also found that the middle class was shrinking, as more people polarized to either end of the income spectrum. By 1996, only 27.5 percent of families were found in what used to be the middle class (i.e., those earning between $31,666 and $55,992 per year). This group used to comprise 40 percent of families. The poorest families, once 10 percent of the population, now were 16.7 percent. The richest went from 10 percent to 18.1 percent. In the U.S., the gap is much more dramatic. Thankfully, Canada's social safety net and progressive taxation system minimized the gap until the neo-cons took hold of the reins of power.

Given the enormous amounts of time, energy, and money spent in convincing us to consume, it is hardly surprising that no one has ever been successful at convincing North American consumers to live a simpler life. Movements for voluntary simplicity, while admirable, are highly unlikely to convince a majority, or even a significant minority, to drop out of consumer society. Fortunately, the new consumer activists have a better idea. They believe that consumer literacy can have an impact on the worst practices of corporations.

Nike is the ultimate corporation of the 1990s: cool, global, and greedy. In fact, it is so cool that its corporate logo, the swoosh, is instantly recognizable, and billboards don't even carry its name any more. Nike pays superstars like basketball legend Michael Jordan and golf wonder Tiger Woods millions to promote its shoes, but it doesn't even pay a living wage to the workers in China, Vietnam, and Indonesia who make those shoes.

In an extraordinary moment in his film *The Big One*, Michael Moore accuses Nike's CEO, Phil Knight, of paying Indonesian workers less than forty cents a day and hiring twelve-year-old workers. "Fourteen," Knight replies, falling into the trap and confirming that the company uses child labour. In 1997, Vietnam Labor Watch, a New York–based organization, reported that Nike workers in Vietnam were paid a daily wage of $1.60 in a country where three simple meals cost $2.10. The workers reported they had to choose between eating and paying their rent. Nike team leaders in Vietnam make a monthly wage of $42. The minimum wage is $45 a month.

Nike has become a lightning rod for human-rights and labour groups. Independent investigations of the company's plants have found abusive working conditions, low wages, and illegally long hours. The CBS show "48 Hours" detailed other abuses in Nike supply factories in Vietnam a couple of years ago. Punished workers were forced to kneel with their hands in the air for twenty-five minutes and a woman had her mouth taped shut for talking. The *Philadelphia Inquirer* reported that in Vietnam on International Women's Day 1998, fifty-six female workers were forced to run around a two-kilometre factory perimeter because they had not worn regulation shoes. A dozen of those women collapsed of heat exhaustion. A report by two Hong Kong–based human-rights groups in the fall of 1998 charged that Nike violates even Chinese labour laws. And a leaked report by the accounting firm Ernst and Young, which was hired by Nike itself to audit its suppliers' factories, found that workers at a factory near Ho Chi Minh City were exposed to carcinogens that exceeded local legal standards by 177 times and that 77 percent of employees suffered from respiratory problems.

Nike has devoted considerable energy to countering this terrible publicity about its labour practices. After all, image is the company's lifeblood. A $90 pair of running shoes has only $1.60 in labour costs; the rest is promotion and profit. But the company still refuses to allow an independent monitoring of its suppliers' factories unless all other sport-shoe manufacturers do the same.

The author Naomi Klein told me in an interview that Nike is also a target because it has totally severed its marketing campaigns from providing jobs in the community. This is nowhere more pronounced than in the inner city. "They are feeding off the culture of black youth in the inner city without providing jobs. They are more in your face and also less protected," she explains.

Of course, Nike isn't the only target of human-rights and labour organizations, and these kinds of transgressions aren't happening only in the Third World. The Clean Clothes campaign, which is directed against corporations who use sweatshop labour in the Third World and at home, has swept American campuses in the past couple of years. Duke University was the first school to adopt a code of conduct to cover all Duke-embossed gear. Believe it or not, 700 contractors were involved in making this gear. In the spring of 1998, the university created a set of tough rules requiring that, among other things, supplier companies pay a living wage and provide full disclosure of their factories, with addresses. This information can then be provided to NGOs (non-governmental organizations), and they start monitoring. The movement spread quickly. By the end of the 1999 school year, sit-ins at various schools demanded similar action. The *New York Times* called it the biggest wave of student protests in twenty years.

To co-opt the movement, and at the urging of the companies targeted, the White House set up a Clean Clothes Task Force. The companies behind the task force would not agree to pay a living wage and would not submit to real monitoring. Then Nike started reaching out to universities and asking them to join the task force; one hundred schools signed on. The result was that the student movement started to get bogged down in bureaucratic wrangling with the companies. Now all the unions and churches involved have stepped down from the task force and students are denouncing it.

Canada's *Adbusters* magazine has played a central role in another part of the anti-consumer movement: culture jamming. This practice seeks to use the very instruments of culture that promote consumerism, primarily the media and advertising, to educate against consumerism. Naomi Klein says that the advertising world has tried to co-opt the critique of advertising. This just makes people even more angry. Anti-ad advertising is everywhere.

Reading *Adbusters*, you'd think the anti-consumer revolution was around the corner, but I have my doubts. Still, Klein warns us not to underestimate this diverse, grass-roots, anti-corporate, anti-consumer movement. "Every time I have thought that this is going to fall apart it has taken itself to the next level. Up until now there has been a feeling that the less centralized and fewer leaders there are, then the less vulnerable you are to co-optation and marginalization. I think next we are going to see some leaders emerge."

In the fall and winter of 1998, I travelled around the country as a commissioner on the Council of Canadians' inquiry into the

Multilateral Agreement on Investment (MAI). The inquiry hit about twelve cities across Canada. In city after city, young people came out to discuss alternatives to corporate globalization. They were not talking about new legislation or this right or that. They were talking about transforming the system of global corporate greed that dominates our lives. It was the most radical talk I had heard in years.

At the Halifax inquiry, a young man active in popular theatre passionately decried the corporate takeover of Nova Scotia's cultural industries. In a letter denouncing someone who supported corporate arts sponsorship, Stephen Cross wrote:

> Downsizing is creating more unemployed Canadians every day. Banks merge and the gap between rich and poor grows, as does the number of people living below the poverty line. And in this toxic environment, you suggest artists should get in bed with these giants of industry because we have something government wants. The ability to create artistic commodities and jobs, jobs, jobs. And who will we be creating these commodities for, the low-income earner or the ruling class? In effect you are advocating that we sell our souls to assimilate into the corporate culture. . . . I believe that the common people of Nova Scotia are being forced out of active participation in the culture of this province in the same way that they have been forced out of participation in the economic processes of this province. This must change.

Just before the Halifax conference, we got news that the MAI had been derailed by the global grass-roots campaign led by the Council of Canadians. At the time of this writing, massive protest at the WTO meetings in Seattle were being compared with the uprising against the war in Vietnam. The victory of the anti-MAI forces and the impressive display of people power in Seattle have given new energy to the international movement against anti-democratic trade deals. The economist Sylvia Ostry, who had been involved with negotiating international trade deals on behalf of the Canadian government for twenty years, said on "Straight from the Hip," my current CBC Newsworld program, "People I work with, including governments, don't know what to do about this global protest movement." Governments and corporations may know how to co-opt national protest movements, but an international movement is another kettle of fish.

Whether they're campus-wide or worldwide, these anti-corporate campaigns contain a strong anti-consumerist, pro-environmental critique, as well as a deep message of democratization. It makes sense that in an age when consumerism and corporate dominance have become the central features of our culture, rebellion against them has created the most vibrant of our social movements.

Collective consumer power can be an effective weapon for social change, but historically it has worked only when the campaign is so massive and so obvious that millions of people support it. The best examples of effective consumer actions were the grape boycotts of the 1960s and 1970s, when farm workers in California organized a stunning campaign under the leadership of the legendary Cesar Chavez and convinced a generation of North Americans not to eat grapes. These campaigns were to support farm workers and migrant labourers in their struggle to unionize and win better working conditions. To this day, I have trouble buying grapes in the supermarket. The sanctions against the South African apartheid government were another successful boycott that combined consumer, corporate, and government action to maximize pressure on a repressive and racist regime. Some anti-corporate movements have had an impact, but they have not yet reached the mass proportions that would be necessary to really change consumer behaviour. What appeals to me most in these campaigns is how they challenge the corporate consumer culture that has become so pervasive in the past two decades and put the finger on corporate greed.

Of course, the cost of consumerism is not only the exploitation of Third World workers, but also the intensification of work and work time for employees everywhere. Consumerism is a trap that focuses your energy on private consumption rather than on public good, but it also sets you on a treadmill that can lead to increased work time. And anyone who works long hours will be unable to participate in society as a fully active citizen.

The average family used to put in fifty-four hours of work a week; today that figure has risen to eighty-six hours. The left usually uses these figures to show how buying power has declined, but it is also true that expectations have risen. Today a simple TV set is not enough — you need surround sound and a Playstation and maybe two or three TVs, one for each generation and gender. Unfortunately, the left has fallen into the trap of arguing that only economic growth can provide the jobs and prosperity we need. But as those in the environmental movement have pointed out, there are limits to how much growth the planet can sustain. To the environmental devastation that comes with limitless growth we have to add human devastation, not only because of the excessive exploitation of people in the developing countries but also because of the excesses of work in the North.

Control over work time, I believe, should be a central economic demand of the new millennium. According to Statistics Canada's *Labour Force Survey*, almost one-fifth of Canadian employees worked overtime during the first quarter of 1997, and most did so without getting extra pay for their additional work. The average amount of overtime was 9.1 hours per week. Quoted in the *Globe and Mail*, Gordon Betcherman, an Ottawa-based economist who specializes in labour market issues, said many workers "have gotten the signal that they have to have a very strong commitment to their work and if they don't there are others out there who will." Many salaried employees are "under tremendous pressure to work long hours and not get paid for it," he added. "In the lean, tough 1990s, the culture of the organization is such that if you need to put in 45 hours to get the project done, you do it."

Of course, most of those working long hours were professionals and managers. For those at the other end of the income scale, the problem is more likely to be too few hours and too little control over hours of work. The same StatsCan study showed that those working part time made up 19 percent of the workforce. While the average number of hours worked has changed little in recent years, the distribution of those hours has changed considerably. There are 11 percent fewer people working a standard thirty-five- to forty-hour work week than there were twenty years ago. The number of non-student workers with shorter hours has tripled in that time, and the number of people working longer hours has also increased.

When "Cross Country Checkup," CBC's national call-in show, asked people about their attitudes towards work, many callers expressed serious concerns about overdoing it. "Most people I know in business are working at work, at home, on the weekend, and at nights," said one caller from Lower Sackville, New Brunswick. "I hate to complain about working too much when so many of my friends and relatives have no work at all."

In its influential report *Good Jobs, Bad Jobs*, the Conference Board of Canada pointed to the polarization in hours worked as a major factor in the separation of good jobs from bad. Part-time work pays less and has fewer benefits, for example, than full-time work. Breaking down the distinctions between full-time and part-time work by providing equal access to benefits and security can help counter this trend. A new Labour Standards Act, passed in Saskatchewan in 1994, requires firms with more than twenty employees to offer part-timers the same benefits, in proportion to hours worked, as full-timers and to give workers at least one week's notice of changes to work schedules. This second provision addresses another important issue: control over work time. According to StatsCan, 22 percent of workers report feeling as if they are "on call" for their employers. "A lot of people say wages are the major issue in the hospitality industry," says Peggy Nash, coordinator of bargaining in the hospitality sector for the Canadian Auto Workers. "I think scheduling hours is at least as big a problem."

Scheduling of hours of work was a central issue at Starbucks, the multinational coffee chain organized by the CAW in Vancouver. "Workers could think they were working thirty hours that week and wind up working eight hours," says Nash. "No one can live like that." At Starbucks, the CAW succeeded in winning a scheduling system that was based partly on seniority and would be more predictable for workers. But a similar proposal to give part-time workers more hours when available was removed from the Saskatchewan Labour Standards Act because of employer opposition.

Two-thirds of part-time workers say no when asked if they would prefer full-time work, and so Statistics Canada calls them "voluntary" part-time workers. For many women, however, such "voluntary" part-time work is the only kind they can sustain because they carry the major responsibility for childcare, elder care, and home management — and cuts to the public service are shifting more of these responsibilities into the home. Thus many women can deal with their overwhelming responsibilities at home only by working part time. Many men, by contrast, deal with the insecurities of work and social services by working longer hours. The result of these trends could very well be a widening of the economic gender gap.

But the effect on income of polarization is only part of the story. As women's status outside the home has developed, the work they do within the home and their communities has become less and less valued. Feminist economists like New Zealand's Marilyn Waring have long argued that women's unpaid labour is vital to our economy. Yet the unpaid work that women do seems never to have had less value than it does today. The myriad strains on today's families and communities have, for a variety of reasons, reached critical proportions in the nineties. But society's failure to value the work of nurturing one's family and community, and the unwillingness to acknowledge the lack of time people have for this work, is a large part of the picture.

Cutting back on hours of work could solve a lot of problems, including unemployment, lack of opportunities for youth, and excessive stress on parents. As someone who has had the freedom and privilege to cut back on my work hours, I can honestly say that no single thing I have done in my life has contributed more to my sense of well-being.

Working long hours is a vicious circle in many ways. Even if your employer doesn't require those long hours, work can be a substitute for other things that are missing from your life. It is easy to avoid dealing with a troubled relationship by escaping to work, for example. Nevertheless, in places where shorter work hours have been tried, people are usually happier, even when income declines as a result.

In 1994, when Lloyd Axworthy, who was at the time human resources minister, was still trying to develop an alternative to the slash-and-burn politics of Finance Minister Paul Martin, he assigned the economist Arthur Donner to pull together an advisory group on working time and the distribution of work. This group's report remains the best work on the issue so far in Canada. The Donner report projected that a four-day, thirty-hour work week would eliminate most of Canada's unemployment, but then decided that such a goal could be reached only gradually, through mostly voluntary changes.

In organizations where such changes have taken place, workers wouldn't have it any other way. A study of four industries in four provinces by the Communications, Energy and Paperworkers Union of Canada found that creating or saving jobs was the primary motivating factor in workers agreeing to a shorter work week, and Statistics Canada surveys confirm this link. In 1986, 17 percent of people surveyed by StatsCan said they would accept a cut in pay with shorter hours if it resulted in job creation and 31 percent said they would give up future wage increases. In 1996, when the question was put without the reference to job creation, only 6 percent said they would accept a pay cut to work shorter hours. Part of the reason for this is the stagnation of incomes over the past ten years, but it is also because the culture of overwork and consumerism has taken an even stronger hold.

Yet once workers experience a shorter work week, quality of life is the reason they want to keep it. As one pulp-and-paper worker in Shawinigan, Quebec, told the CEP Union, "We look at it that we have more time off than [similar workers across Canada] do. . . . They are going to have more TV sets or telephones or whatever. More money does not necessarily increase your quality of life." These ideas were echoed in British Columbia by an employee of the *Kamloops Daily News*. "I asked, Why am I doing this? Why am I killing myself? You have all this stuff and all you have to do is repair it. Now we have less stuff but more fun."

But having more fun isn't the only reason to work less. People interviewed in the study also found that shorter work weeks allowed more time for involvement in the community, a union, or a political party, as well as for family. "The less overtime you do, the less you want to do," said another worker at the Shawinigan mill. "You adjust your budget, have a new, quiet life, get involved in outside activities. And once you get involved, you want to go ahead and do it every week."

At the Polysar Rubber Company in Sarnia, Ontario, the union negotiated a small reduction in work time by taking every third Friday off. These became known as Happy Fridays, and they were so popular that other workplaces picked them up. Now Happy Fridays are a community event, with family picnics, fishing derbies, and golf tournaments. Shops and restaurants hire extra staff to handle the business.

In Europe, shorter work weeks have become a central demand of the labour movement and a platform feature of every left-of-centre party. In France, the work week is being reduced from thirty-nine to thirty-five hours through a combination of legislation and financial incentives to employers. The first of two thirty-five-hour laws, the Aubry law, was approved in May 1998. The law mandates a thirty-five-hour work week as the legislated standard as of January 1, 2000. Significant financial incentives in the form of lower payroll taxes will be provided for companies that reduce hours and hire more workers. The sooner a company reduces hours, the more generous the aid. In Italy, the work week will be reduced from forty hours to thirty-five by 2001 in a similar manner. Other countries like the Netherlands, Belgium, and Denmark have also moved in the direction of shorter work time. It is a major issue in Europe, but in Canada the only moves are in the opposite direction.

Shorter work time — or, as I prefer to call it, control over work time — speaks to many problems in our society. More time for both moms and dads would help solve the crisis of family that women feel so acutely. The extreme polarization of work hours and therefore income could be significantly reduced. Opportunities for younger people who are stuck in non-standard jobs would open up. And shorter work hours could give us the immediate positive reinforcement we need to give up the quest for more consumer goods in favour of a better lifestyle. Most important, shorter work time would give more citizens the freedom to fully participate in the democratic process.

The push for shorter work time has long been a cornerstone of the labour movement. In Canada, there was a widespread campaign for a nine-hour day as early as 1872. In the United States, on April 6, 1933, the Senate passed a labour-backed bill mandating a thirty-hour week in most industries. The bill's sponsor, Senator Hugo Black of Alabama, called the thirty-hour week the "only practical and possible method of dealing with unemployment." In the face of business opposition, however, the bill became stalled in the House of Representatives. It was eventually supplanted by President Franklin Roosevelt's New Deal legislation, which attempted to reduce unemployment through public works and economic growth rather than shorter hours.

Even some long-ago employers promoted shorter work weeks as a way of creating jobs. Most notable was W. K. Kellogg, the quirky cereal magnate of Battle Creek, Michigan, who introduced a thirty-hour week in his factory in 1930. Though it was initially very popular, the shorter work week at Kellogg's was gradually eroded after the Second World War and finally abandoned in 1984.

In general, while a call for shorter hours remained part of trade-union policy, there was little enthusiasm for it in the postwar period.

Instead, labour bought into the prevailing idea that the route to happiness was to create jobs and gain access to more of the goodies of consumer society through economic growth. Maybe the time has come for labour to return to the old idea of bread and roses. We want bread (more money), but we want roses (a better quality of life), too. To achieve a better quality of life, time is just as important as money. And time is a critical factor in reinventing democracy to include a larger number of participants.

10

The Media Are the Message

IN THE SPRING OF 1998, I CHAIRED a discussion with the two highest-profile and most respected anchors in Canada. Peter Mansbridge, anchor of the CBC national news, and Lloyd Robertson, anchor of the CTV national news, answered questions from journalists as part of the Canadian Association of Journalists (CAJ) convention. A woman asked why women hadn't made more progress, and in particular why so few women were used as sources for media stories. Studies done by Media Watch in Canada and the Feminist Majority in the United States show that women are about 15 percent of those quoted in media stories, and that the vast majority of women quoted are victims of crime rather than experts. Peter Mansbridge responded by talking about the transformation in the participation of women in the newsroom since he started in the business. He avoided the question about women sources.

The week before that CAJ conference, the Multilateral Agreement on Investment had been successfully sidetracked by a grass-roots citizens' movement led in no small measure by Maude Barlow and her Council of Canadians. The media had missed the story, and most people on the left assumed that this was because of corporate ownership of the media and the interest of business in the MAI. And there was some truth to this. But a more important factor was the way in which journalists learn to filter the world. They missed the story because they did not take the Council of Canadians seriously. In fact, they have written off citizens' groups as a force in society. When Maude Barlow's name is mentioned, a lot of journalists roll their eyes. "She has no credibility," one journalist told me. "No one wants to use her." Credibility with whom? I asked. Hundreds of thousands of people across Canada see Barlow as a leader of their movement. Her books sell thousands of copies. She is constantly on the lecture tour. She has earned tremendous respect around the world for her leadership. But the media in Canada don't see her as credible because the power she exercises is collective power, not the individual power of business leaders or politicians. And this is not just about Maude Barlow.

They had the same reaction to me during the Charlottetown Accord, when I was president of NAC. Every time I walked into a room with journalists during the marathon negotiations that resulted in Charlottetown, I saw the rolling of eyes. Pressure groups like the Council of Canadians and NAC are acceptable when they keep their place: a protest against a government bill here, a lobby against a government bill there. But when an advocacy group actually finds itself in a position to challenge power in a significant way, the media will almost always marginalize it. It's like a sexist male's attitude to an uppity woman.

When I challenged Peter Mansbridge on the lack of women sources, he replied that it had nothing to do with rolling eyes. He explained that in the newsroom of "The National," they had had a discussion when I was president of NAC about using "spokespeople" (he used his fingers to put quotes around the term) all the time, concluded that these people say the same thing over and over again, and so decided not to use them any more as sources. If saying things over and over disqualified people from talking on the media, we would have empty screens and blank newspaper pages. Politicians and pundits are more predictable than the most dogmatic advocacy group spokesperson. But the most revealing part of Mansbridge's response was the way he put quotation marks around the word "spokespeople." As I explained earlier, an important part of the right-wing shift is to undermine the credibility of advocacy groups and unions. This shift has profoundly affected the media. Citizens' groups are credible only when the politicians give them credibility by responding to their demands. Unless you have an unbelievably compelling and new story to tell, the only other way to get attention is by disruption.

In the 1999 Ontario election, for example, advocacy groups found that the only way to bring attention to their issues was to organize a rowdy demonstration against Premier Mike Harris. Press conferences, even reports on education or poverty, got very little attention. The focus is on the leaders, the journalists would explain. Elections used to be a time when public discussion of political issues was greatly expanded. Advocacy groups were able to raise issues through questioning politicians, issuing report cards on government activity, and participating in all-candidates debates, which were often covered in the local media. Over the past decade, however, media reports about issues in election campaigns have been seriously reduced. The horse race based on polling becomes one focus of election coverage and the well-orchestrated photo-op campaigns of the leaders the other. Even the leaders' debates have been reduced to sound clips without much substantive policy discussion.

Protests have always been a way for advocacy groups to bring attention to their issues during elections, but over the past decade they have become practically the only way. David Peterson was defeated in 1990 in no small measure because protests against him grew to such proportions that there appeared to be a tidal wave of opposition. In the last Ontario election, protesters reminded voters how much chaos Mike Harris's heavy-handed government had created. The Tories spent millions in pre-election propaganda trying to make people forget how confrontational, ideological, and hard-line their government is. The protesters reminded us.

But even the public space for protesting is being limited. Harris's appearances were tightly controlled to exclude any unplanned contact with people. You had to be very well organized to even find him, let alone get access to him. Still, what protests there were were angrier because Harris has excluded so many citizens' groups from his governing of Ontario. There were an unprecedented twelve arrests during the 1999 election campaign. There had never been a single arrest in a previous Ontario election.

The limitations placed on the rights of protesters during the APEC meetings in Vancouver in 1997 are another example of the way in which globalization and neo-liberalism are reducing the public space for democratic dialogue and debate. In that case, the possible involvement of the PMO in the police repression of protesters made this denial of democratic rights a major and long-term national issue.

Whether you're an advocate or a politician, only power or the smell of it will get you attention. This is part of the pressure populist parties feel to move more to the mainstream. The NDP, on the one hand, and Reform, on the other, get attention only for being close to power or from looking like they are making the changes necessary to get closer to power. That's why the media were so fascinated by the machinations of the Unite the Right story, and why they finally paid attention to Alexa McDonough only after she said that her party would be more open to small business.

Journalism is about selecting information, and inevitably there will be bias in that selection. The extraordinary thing is how often that bias generalizes throughout the mainstream media. This is a process that the Italian philosopher Antonio Gramsci called hegemony. It is the process by which a liberal democracy ensures that those in a position of power reproduce the ideas that maintain the status quo. I notice the pressure myself. Clearly my role in the media is to present a left-wing opinion. That's what I get paid for, and no one ever pressures me to change my views. However, if I write a column on the hot news item of that week, it will get better play than if I write about something that hasn't made the news. To be fair, the prominence is also related to the quality of the column. But the subtle pressure on me is still to write about what everyone else is writing about. I may have a different point of view about it, but I jump on the bandwagon of defining "what's important." Even though I am conscious of this process, I still often write about a top news item because I like getting more attention for my column. As I said, it is a very subtle process.

It can also be more obvious, however. A veteran journalist from southwestern Ontario told the CAJ convention that she had proposed a series of stories about privatization and its impact on the Kitchener-Waterloo community. She had been writing for twenty years, so she knew how to craft a good story. Her idea was turned down. It was boring, said her editor. Her experience has been that every time she proposes a story that is outside conventional economic and political wisdom, it is turned down. Reporters know what they have to do to get their stories accepted, and to get them on the national news or the front page. If they want to further their careers, they will do what their editors or producers want them to do.

The change in the media's attitude towards advocacy groups is just one example of how this process works. When I was president of NAC, advocacy groups from Greenpeace to the Assembly of First Nations got a lot of media attention. The Reform Party and the right wing of the federal Conservatives were the first to begin a campaign against these "special-interest groups." The focus at first was on government funding for these groups, but the real target was their credibility. Barbara McDougall, who was at one time minister responsible for women's issues in the Mulroney government and is herself a feminist, would say over and over again that she was a member of the YWCA to swim, not to support NAC, thus undermining NAC's claims on representation. The Reform Party waged a long campaign attacking the funding of groups like NAC under the rubric of fiscal responsibility. Given that NAC, even at its height, never received more than $750,000 from the federal government, the campaign was never really about money: it was about credibility. Groups like NAC were the most effective opposition to right-wing ideas in the country. It was NAC with its 1987 Get the Budget Back on Track campaign, for example, that first drew attention to the right turn of the Mulroney government. It was various advocacy groups that pointed out every right-wing yahoo in the ranks of the Reform Party. Clearly, the right wing needed to undermine the credibility of advocacy groups in order to succeed in imposing its agenda. After the Charlottetown Accord, the media were finally convinced to go along, as Peter Mansbridge's comments illustrate.

The homogeneity on deficit hysteria is an even clearer example of how the media act in the interest of the economic elite. The left helped to create the problem by refusing to recognize at first that there was a fiscal crisis. But the deficit was real; it wasn't made up. It was a problem that we were paying forty cents on every dollar to the banks. By the time Linda McQuaig's book *Shooting the Hippo* came out in 1996, and she explained that the deficit was created by high interest rates and unemployment rather than social spending, it was too late to turn around the universal elite opinion that the deficit could be reduced only by spending cuts.

One of the things the right has been able to do is paint the left as big spenders. Those on the right define themselves as being fiscally responsible and in favour of small government, and they define the left as being big spenders and pro–big government. Well, that's not how I think of the left — not even the social-democratic left. In fact, fiscal responsibility has nothing to do with right and left. But we let them define the debate that way, and that was very weak ground for us because no one wants big-spending, irresponsible government.

Yet even though the left bears some responsibility here, the media have been completely unbalanced in their reporting of fiscal matters. In 1999, for example, when the only two governments left with a deficit were those in B.C. and Ontario, the difference in the media criticism of each was dramatic. Ontario's deficit should have been a much more serious problem, especially for fiscal conservatives, because it was so much greater and because the province continued to run a deficit despite booming economic times. Yet Glen Clark's NDP government was under much greater attack for its fiscal irresponsibility than Mike Harris's Tory government ever was. The reason is clearly that Harris's policy of reducing social spending, weakening labour standards, and cutting taxes benefited the economic elites. Deficit hysteria had little to do with the problem of the deficit, in fact, and everything to do with restructuring the state to benefit the economic elites.

Although it is clear why private media owners have an interest in supporting such policies, it is harder to understand why the average journalist does. With the exception of some highly paid media stars, most working journalists would find that their personal economic and social interests correspond more closely to those of the average working person than of the economic elites. Yet the pressure on journalists to accept the version of reality served up by those elites through their think-tanks, political parties, and academic ideologues is enormous.

The dominance of right-wing pundits in the media is another example of the right-wing bias. In an article in *How Ottawa Spends 1989–90*, Frank Graves points out "that the plurality of Canadians (around 40 percent) identify themselves as small-l liberals and about one in four identify themselves as small-c conservatives. By contrast, in the U.S. less than 8 percent of the public will accept a liberal label." Think about the columnists you read in your newspaper or the commentators you see on television or hear on radio, and then think about what percentage of them are small-c conservative.

I was listening to a CBC interview with the feminist political scientist Barbara Cameron in the spring of 1998. The interview was about a census statistic that had just been released and showed that the most common jobs were truck driver for men and retail sales clerk for women. In fact, almost all the jobs in the top ten were working class. "Where did all the high-tech jobs go?" asked the interviewer, with astonishment in her voice. Cameron hesitated for a moment and then answered, "Well, the high-tech jobs are there, but they aren't as numerous as people seem to think. The picture of what jobs people have hasn't really changed all that much."

It was really striking. Where in the media would you ever get the idea that most people work as janitors, cashiers, and truck drivers? The media actively creates an image of reality where middle-class professionals, both male and female, dominate. And the CBC interviewer's question reflects the fact that most journalists believe that image. It is a reproduction of their own reality, of course, but it is also more insidious than that.

In the summer of 1997, the writer and editor Robert Chodos and I decided to write an article concerning shorter work time, an issue that interests both of us. Ken Whyte, who was then the editor of *Saturday Night*, had told me he was interested in my writing for the magazine, so I had lunch with him to talk about our idea. Whyte indicated that he had a similar concern. He said he had noticed how little time his neighbours seemed to have for simple pleasures like reading. All people seem to do, he said to me, is work or shop. So Robert and I began work on our article. We were well aware that *Saturday Night* usually focuses on the concerns of urban professionals, so we were sure to include some of those concerns in our article, but we concentrated a lot of our attention on working-class people. For one thing, unions have done more work on shorter work time than almost any other organization. For another, one of the more interesting experiments in shorter work time took place at the Kellogg factory in Michigan. And finally, we actually interviewed a Chinese immigrant woman who was working twelve hours a day, six days a week, at below the minimum wage in a Toronto sweatshop.

We submitted the article. After a long delay, Whyte wrote me, rejecting our piece. "The more personal material on boomers opting out of the rat race was what originally intrigued me most," he explained. "I understood the story was to be about how the two of you, like a lot of others, felt that careerism wasn't enough and that other options were increasingly appealing."

Now, I think personal journalism can be appealing too. And it is true that Chodos and I have both come to issues around working time through our own experiences, which we could have talked about in the article. But he and I are hardly representative of most people's reality. We have infinitely more choices than most people. To write an article on shorter work time based on our personal experiences might be entertaining, but it would have very little to do with looking at how policy changes can affect the lives of the people who are suffering the most under this economy. And this is what we wanted to do.

Saturday Night was not interested in reflecting most people's everyday reality. Yet the problem is not only that the lives of ordinary people are rarely reflected, but also that their economic interests are rarely presented. The best example of this is the debate on tax cuts. The debate about tax cuts is perhaps the most misleading of any in the media. The Fraser Institute, and other organizations like it, has convinced us that we pay 50 percent of our income towards taxes. Their Tax Freedom Day suggests that we work half the year for the government and only half the year for ourselves. From a public-relations point of view the gimmick is brilliant, but it has nothing to do with reality. Indeed, I was always pretty suspicious of these figures because I know that I make a higher-than-average income and pay nowhere near 50 percent of it in taxes.

The CAW economist Jim Stanford has discerned the actual figures by looking at Revenue Canada reports. The average income of the almost 21 million Canadians who filed tax returns for 1996 was just over $26,000. A full 60 percent reported a total income of less than $25,000 for the year. Those 21 million tax filers paid federal and provincial income taxes and surtaxes totalling just 18 percent of their income. For an individual with a truly average income of $26,000, the effective income tax rate was about 13 percent. Even when taxes such as property and sales taxes are included, the total rate paid by middle-income Canadians rarely exceeds 25 percent. For Canadians in the $50,000 to $60,000 bracket, the tax rate was a modest 21.5 percent.

One can understand why the ideologically driven Fraser Institute would fudge its tax figures, but why hasn't the media unearthed the real story?

The more journalists reproduce their own reality, the less the majority of people — the working class and the poor — see themselves and their lives reflected in the media. And even more important, the less the needs of the majority get examined. And if you think showing the lives of the average person is not interesting or entertaining, have a look at *The Full Monty* or *Secrets and Lies* or some of the fantastic documentaries produced in this country. Or look at the *Toronto Star*'s coverage of the 1998 federal election by Tom Walkom, who spent most of the campaign travelling around the country talking to ordinary citizens. His articles were more interesting and informative than those of the whole Ottawa press gallery put together.

The only time we see the lives of ordinary people reflected is during disasters or in some public-interest features or through polls. The media-reflected reality is that of upper-middle-class Canadians. The simple fact that all news networks flash stock-market quotes rather than the prices of food is evidence of this false picture of what's important to most people.

A lot has been written about the corporate concentration of media in Canada. In fact, Canada has the most highly concentrated media industry in the world. One man owns the majority of newspapers in the country, and television and radio ownership is almost as concentrated. Just ten companies control 55 percent of the revenue in the radio industry, an increase of 50 percent in the past decade alone. Television is even more concentrated.

Efforts to limit media concentration have failed utterly. In 1969, Senator Keith Davey called for an investigation into the ownership of Canada's media after discovering that the Irving family had gained control of every English-language daily in New Brunswick. The resulting committee, the Senate Committee on Mass Media, recommended in 1970 that the federal government set up a Press

Ownership Review Board to represent the public interest in future newspaper mergers. In 1971, a lower court ordered the Irving family to give up their Moncton paper after the federal government charged contravention of the Combines Investigation Act. A higher court overturned the ruling. In the next few years, Thomson and Southam also began building their empires and consolidating newspapers. The *Toronto Telegram, Montreal Star, Ottawa Journal,* and *Winnipeg Tribune* closed down. Later Hollinger, the Sun chain, and Quebecor entered the picture. In 1970, independents owned 41.5 percent of newspapers. By 1996, they owned only 17 percent. The evolution of capitalism towards mergers and bigger and bigger companies has massively affected the communications industry.

Nevertheless, as someone who has worked for a public broadcaster over the past several years, I understand that corporate concentration is only part of the reason why the media reflect such a distorted reality. A much more important reason is the commercialization of the media. As the Canadian political scientist Colin Leys points out in his article on the media in the 1999 *Socialist Register:* "Focusing on the issue of how many owners there were has often tended to obscure the fact that market competition ultimately obliges all owners of mass-circulation newspapers [and mainstream TV and radio stations] to run them as a business, not as a service to democracy. Survival depends on readership maximization, and readership maximization depends on entertainment — not political debate. . . . The ideal of the 'collective conversation' of a national society is increasingly displaced by that of a multiplicity of individuals passively viewing the world through the eyes of global business." This is nowhere clearer than in our so-called newspaper wars, where the personal day-to-day experience of hip, young journalists (what *Maclean's* magazine calls "I Journalism") is displacing serious political commentary.

Leys also shows how the drive for ever-increasing profits has reinforced the market orientation of the media. According to Leys, the journalism staff on U.S. dailies fell by almost a quarter and on weeklies by more than a third in the ten years between 1982 and

1992. In Britain, the total editorial staffing of all papers is estimated to have fallen by at least 40 percent between 1977 and 1993, while the total number of pages per issue has increased by 72 percent.

When you are strapped for time, it is hard to do original research for a story and even harder not to use the same tried and true talking heads from the Rolodex. The solution lies in developing alternative models of journalism to pressure all media, both public and private, to carry out a form of journalism that will facilitate, rather than restrict, citizen participation.

The organizations that will have the most important part in democratizing the media will be the public broadcasters, and in particular the CBC. During major political debates in this country, the CBC often already plays the role of enabling citizen participation. For example, during the Charlottetown Accord, CBC Newsworld televised the citizens' forums and "The National" held a series of broad panel discussions, which included some citizen participation. The network also sponsored impressive citizens' forums on the constitution and the budget.

I was particularly struck by the special "72 Hours to Remake Canada," broadcast by the CBC in 1997. The network selected a group of about twenty Canadians who were regionally, politically, and demographically representative. Their task was to create the basis for a new constitutional agreement within seventy-two hours. I remember one fellow who was from southern Alberta and, as one would expect, quite hostile to Quebec. Over the course of the event, his hostility completely disappeared. It became clear that most of it had been based on ignorance. Similarly, the two francophone sovereigntist women learned a lot about what the issues of the English Canadians really were. The group had access to three constitutional experts and were addressed by diverse groups of "players" from the constitutional wars. Within hours, the participants started to identify common interests during meetings held on the budget and Quebec/Canada relations. As has happened with other exercises in participatory democracy, citizens proved more willing to dialogue than politicians and interest-group representatives usually are. They came up with an agreement that was remark-ably similar to the agreement we had hammered out in 1992, in the citizens' constitutional forums leading up to the Charlottetown Accord.

One of the producers of the special assured me that the partici-pants were not manipulated in any way. They actually arrived at their conclusions by listening to each other and trying to arrive at a solution that would best meet everyone's needs. I found watching the process truly inspiring, but the pundits dismissed it as unreal-istic. It seems that every time even a little democracy peeks through the political process, it is branded as unrealistic. The elites who want to maintain their control of the political system can't afford to allow citizen participation to go very far.

The famous CBC town hall meeting during which a nurse took on Jean Chrétien over his record on unemployment insurance is another example of the CBC bringing citizens in on the democratic process. Chrétien has refused to be interviewed by Peter Mansbridge ever since, because Mansbridge saw it as his role to make sure that the PM answered all the questions posed by citizens. The fact that Chrétien's refusal to appear on the flagship national news show never itself became a news item gives you some idea of how cosy the parliamentary press gallery can get with the party in power.

My own network, Newsworld, has also taken some important steps in broadening media coverage. It chooses special days and goes out into the community to look at a targeted issue. Instead of giving more airtime to the usual talking heads, each program is asked to take its cameras out of the studio and into the streets and community centres. The first day like this took a powerful look at Vancouver's downtown East Side. Another one looked at health care and yet another at Native issues. Watching one of these spe-cial days makes so clear how poor day-to-day media coverage is at reflecting the reality of Canadians. These are the kinds of initia-tives we need more of.

In the U.S., media activism is much more advanced than it is in Canada, partly because the media there are far more corrupt.

Fairness and Accuracy in Reporting (FAIR) is an organization of journalists and others who monitor the media for bias and misrepresentation. In addition to local and national campaigns to pressure media outlets on this or that issue, FAIR produces its own radio show, "Counterspin," which is heard on National Public Radio. In Canada, Media Watch, a feminist media watchdog, has had considerable success in campaigning against sexism in the media.

Most media critics in Canada have focused on challenging corporate concentration in general and, more specifically, the cookie monster of Canadian newspapers, Conrad Black. As I said earlier, such challenges have met with little success. But the right-wing Fraser Institute has had considerable influence in challenging what it believes is a liberal bias in the media. A progressive watchdog group like FAIR could have an important impact on the Canadian media. Using the CUB method, it could acquire a broad base of support by requiring all newspapers and cable stations to include a flyer once a year inviting subscribers to join.

Even more useful would be a citizens' board for the CBC. Instead of being filled with patronage appointments, the board should be open to all citizens and possibly elected. Some members could have expertise in communications, culture, and journalism; some in business and politics. Others will be selected because they are generally representative of the viewing and listening public. Members of the employees' unions should also be on the board.

At the moment, the CBC board is composed almost entirely of members of the corporate elite. Given that, is it any wonder that the network often reflects the same politics as the private-sector media? A more democratic, representative, and independent board would be a major step towards making the CBC more accountable. The network president should be hired by the board through a transparent selection process, and the chairperson should be elected by the board. Moreover, its meetings should be public, except where personnel issues are involved. The CBC board could travel across the country and hear from viewers and listeners about the changes they want to see in the network, and citizen advisory boards could also be established to monitor the network and provide feedback on programming.

While all this is going on, we should also implement the most important change: funding to the CBC should be increased so that the network is not reliant on advertisers. Although advertisers don't usually interfere with the editorial content of programming, their interest in particular audiences skews the focus of the network. Moreover, advertisers are usually not that interested in sponsoring programs that challenge the status quo. The heavy presence of business news on CBC Newsworld is one sign of how advertisers can influence programming on a public network.

The CRTC should also be democratized. Anyone who has ever participated in a CRTC hearing knows that the words "bureaucracy" and "red tape" are given new meaning by the massive amounts of documentation required for the hearings. Still, the cross-Canada CRTC hearings on the CBC in early 1999 were an excellent initiative, if only because the CRTC commissioners found out that Canadians really do care about the CBC despite the constant attacks against it in the private media. Why couldn't the CRTC hold such hearings on the private broadcasters as well? They may be privately owned, but they are using public airways. Newspapers present a thornier problem because they are entirely in the private sector.

I often wonder why members of the media aren't more concerned about the low esteem in which they are held by the public. In an Ekos poll, 79 percent of people thought the media had a lot of power and only 34 percent thought they should have more. The only group that fared as badly was big business. Only 68 percent said the federal government had a lot of power. Thirty-seven percent said the media were doing a worse job than five years ago, with only 24 percent thinking they were doing a better job.

In the U.S., a number of newspapers, taking note of the low esteem in which the public holds journalists, have been moving towards what they call civic journalism. Civic journalism is about making connections between journalists and the communities they cover, and between journalism and citizenship. Journalists attempt to reconnect with citizens, improve public discussion, and strengthen civic culture. In 1990, the *Wichita Eagle* in Kansas began its Your Vote Counts project. The paper polled Kansans to determine which issues were most important to them, and then the editors chose to focus their election coverage on twelve of these issues. In partnership with the ABC affiliate KAKE-TV, the *Eagle* also promoted voter registration and turnout.

A second Knight-Ridder paper, the *Charlotte Observer*, teamed with its local ABC affiliate to abandon horse-race coverage in the 1992 elections. A "citizens' agenda" was formed from an initial poll and extensive community-wide interviews. This agenda included issues such as the economy and taxes, crime and drugs, health care, education, the environment, and a general feeling that support structures for family and community life were waning. A citizens' panel of 500 poll respondents monitored the *Observer*'s election coverage to make sure it focused on the citizens' agenda.

Buzz Merritt, the editor of the *Wichita Eagle*, said in 1994:

> The public journalist's newspaper is doing what the conscientious citizen would do given the time and resources to do it: establishing the facts; assaying the problem; sharing thoughts and ideas with other conscientious citizens; resolving underlying issues, such as core values; learning more from successes than failures; aggressively fostering a necessarily noisy but civil discussion leading to a democratic consensus.

Public journalists have gone beyond simply identifying election priorities — they have taken community problems and tried to find solutions by talking with people at a grass-roots level. In Akron, Ohio, for example, the *Beacon Journal*'s five-part project "A Question of Race" won the 1994 Pulitzer Prize. The paper convened focus groups of blacks and whites, and then had these groups observed by reporters. Discussion centred on quantitative data showing continuing disparities between the races; it became very clear that racism was alive and well. With the last part of the series, the paper invited readers to send in a coupon pledging to fight racism. More than 22,000 responded, and half of those had become involved in race-relations projects by the summer of 1994.

Public journalism encourages the journalist to see his or her readers as citizens rather than as consumers. Instead of focusing exclusively on leaders and pundits, media outlets interested in public journalism seek ways of both informing and being informed by people in their community. In this way, they come to see that their role in preserving and extending democracy is absolutely central. The problem with it is that it fails to recognize the class bias in the media and the restrictions inherent in private ownership.

Unfortunately, a lot of people on the left have given up on the idea of ever seeing the mainstream media reflect a diversity of views. They focus their energy instead on alternative media. In the U.S., where the process of shutting out almost any left-wing view is much more advanced than it is in Canada, there is a large and thriving alternative media. Canadian alternatives like *This Magazine*, *Canadian Forum*, and *Canadian Dimension*, as well as numerous feminist and community newspapers and radio stations, also play an important role in informing and reflecting the interests of their communities, but they rarely have any influence on the mainstream media, which is what most people rely on for their information and views.

The exception to this could be the Internet. Just as the Gulf War made CNN an indispensable information source, so the NATO bombing of Yugoslavia showed what an effective source of news and views the Internet can be. The old adage that the first casualty of war is the truth may be dumped in the dustbin of history by electronic communications. From the moment of the first bombings, I started to get e-mails of articles providing an alternative to the mainstream media. Anyone could have logged on to numerous alternative Web sites to find out what the mainstream news outlets wouldn't print. After the first day of bombing, for example, I logged on to Z *Magazine*'s wonderful Web site to get three different progressive views of what was going on in Kosovo.

The Internet is also a powerful force because of its interactive nature. I am always amazed by the amount of feedback I get on the Internet. I get more mail from readers of my CBC Online column, for example, than for anything else I have ever done in the media. Indeed, there is an interactive culture on the Internet that just doesn't exist in other media. You might be surprised to learn how many people call television shows like "Face Off," particularly when something pisses them off. On the Internet, however, the mail is of a higher quality. Whenever I wrote a column on a controversial topic, people would write and take issue with one or more of my points, or just write to tell me they agreed with me. Ken Wolff, who runs the Newsworld Web site, tells me that he is convinced that the Internet will change the nature of journalism. When you write a story about a struggle or a community and immediately hear from the people involved about the accuracy of your story, accountability is much more possible. Journalists can actually enter into a direct dialogue with their readers in a way that was simply not possible before.

Alternative publications like Z *Magazine* can also have much wider distribution through the Internet. I had never bought the magazine, for example, but I found their coverage of Kosovo to be indispensable. I have since subscribed to their e-mail commentary service. Nevertheless, access to the Internet is still limited by income and, to a decreasing degree, by gender.

Fundamentally, however, the Internet suffers from the same structural problems as the rest of the media. As the media critic Robert W. McChesney points out in his book *Rich Media, Poor Democracy*, the Internet is just as subject to monopoly control as other types of media are. While distribution problems are not as severe on the Internet as they are in print, it is difficult for alternative media to reach out beyond the usual networks. Just because it is easy to put up a Web site doesn't mean that anyone will visit it. According to McChesney, even major search engines like Yahoo! are using traditional media to advertise, "otherwise an Internet Web site would get lost among the millions of other Web locations." Moreover, it is the media giants that are able to buy prime real estate on major portals like AOL, for example. "The new Microsoft Internet Explorer 4.0 offers 250 highlighted channels, and the plum positions belong to Disney and Time Warner." Most Internet users begin from one of the major commercial portals, such as America Online or Sympatico. In fact, AOL already accounts for 40 percent of all online traffic and 60 percent of home use in the U.S. According to McChesney, more than 80 percent of AOL users never leave the AOL sites.

Links are a powerful new way to reach audiences, but there is no guarantee that mainstream media sites, which are heavily advertised, will provide links to alternative sites any more than mainstream media outlets will provide access to alternative voices. The Internet suffers from the same structural problems as the rest of the media: private ownership, commercialization, and monopoly control.

Nevertheless, the Internet does open up significant new possibilities for alternative media, including television and radio broadcasting.

Despite the importance of alternative media, I have always been of the view that out groups in society have to fight to be represented in the mainstream media. In fact, media representation is an essential requirement of the democratic process. Our public dialogue and debate takes place primarily through the media, and it is essential that a diversity of views be fully represented for democracy to work.

Most progressive groups have a passive-aggressive relationship with the media. I don't know how many discussions I have had with members of different groups who are furious that media outlets cover their issues badly or don't cover them at all, but have no strategy on how to influence the media.

Businesses and governments spend millions trying to influence and manipulate the media. In fact, spin doctors have a much more insidious influence on media bias than corporate concentration does. In almost every struggle and on almost every issue, journalists are bombarded by the perspective of the right, the corporate sector, and the government. Businesses and governments devote considerable resources to developing their communications strategies, and so should the left. Right now, however, these groups often spend more time on internal newsletters than on developing a media strategy.

Part of the reason for this is the cynicism about the media. What is the point of developing a media strategy, the argument goes, if you don't get coverage anyway? Yet when "Face Off" was a daily show, our producers were often unable to locate a spokesperson for a particular group. "We'll discuss it and get back to you," someone would say, then call back two days later. On a daily show, we do not have the luxury of that much time. Every journalist I have ever talked to expressed the same frustrations about dealing with progressive groups.

The notable exception to the rule is the Canadian Auto Workers. Jane Armstrong, who runs the CAW communications department, tells me that she really saw how important a media strategy was during the 1997 Canadian Airlines dispute. Reporters in Alberta seemed quite hostile to the union position at first, but instead of just accepting this, CAW people spent time explaining their side of the issue, providing background information, etc. Within a couple of days, they were able to turn around the media coverage.

Of course, media bias cannot always be turned around. Sometimes journalists seem incapable of understanding an issue. This was my experience around the issue of racism in the women's movement, for example. Other times, corporate ownership does make a direct difference, as evidenced by the failure of the media to report on NAFTA and the MAI.

But on most issues, progressive voices can be heard in the media. It takes strategy, it takes skill, and it takes work. Just as most activists are prepared to put a lot of time and energy into organizing demonstrations, even if their impact is not immediately apparent, so should we be willing to put time and energy into media strategy. It might not pay off immediately, but it will over time, as contacts and credibility are built.

In October 1996, I was on a panel with the Brazilian activist Fernanda Carvalho of the Citizens' Action Campaign against Hunger and for Life. Most of the leaders of the campaign had been in exile or underground during the Brazilian dictatorship and had to struggle mightily against self-marginalization in the democratic period. They built a massive campaign mostly by getting their message out through the media. Carvalho told the conference how Brazil's largest TV station, with its audience of 20 million, wanted to interview her group. She called the man who was the expert on the topic and told him she would send the TV crew right over for the interview. He said he was too busy finishing a document he was writing; he didn't have time to do the interview. This mentality — that it is more important to write a document that will be read by fifty comrades than it is to speak to 20 million Brazilians — is the death of a mass movement, she explained.

Our version of this problem is media cynicism. What is the point of doing the interview, since journalists will distort what we say anyway? Corporate concentration or no, we have to find the ways to make our voices heard through the mass media. Democracy requires no less.

The fundamental problem with the media is that it is privately owned. These days, almost everyone who can afford to own a newspaper shares a common view from the corporate boardrooms. Ideally there would be public funding for independent non-profit media that would reflect a diversity of views. In the immediate, the newspaper councils that exist to hear complaints about bias and include laypeople as well as professional journalists could be expanded to be more proactive. Such councils could, like the

CRTC, travel across the country and hear from citizens about what they want in their newspapers. Public accountability sessions with editors and publishers could be another step in building more accountability into the system. The argument that the market decides is close to nonsense. I buy the *National Post* even though I hate the paper's politics because it has so much more money than the other papers that it can afford to do more investigative journalism.

There must be more pressure on the media to more accurately reflect both political debate and the reality of people's lives. However privately owned the media may be, they have a public trust that even Conrad Black recognizes. The mass media are the only way we have to talk to each other. Those who feel excluded by the mainstream media have to place a greater priority on both learning how to get their stories covered and pressuring the media to cover a greater diversity of stories and issues. The first step, I believe, should be the democratization of the CBC and the CRTC.

11

MONEY IS POWER

NINE TEACHERS SIT AROUND A GIANT GREEN TABLE talking about their pension plan. At first, the enthusiasm is palpable. All of them feel confident about the ability of their pension plan to provide them with a secure future. Feeling secure about retirement in this day and age is a rare privilege, and the teachers are enthusiastic. With assets of more than $40 billion, the Ontario Teachers Pension Plan is the largest, and probably the fastest-growing, private pension plan in the country.

Then the facilitator asks about how the pension fund invests its money. I'm just watching this exchange on videotape, but even I can sense the uncomfortable silence.

"It's a moral dilemma," offers one man, "because downsizing creates a good bottom line, but the criticism is that it doesn't create jobs for young people."

"And where do you stand?" asks the facilitator.

"I think it will become a growing issue, as it gets more publicity, that the teachers pension plan is investing in companies that are downsizing and screwing other unions," he replies.

"Is it an issue for you?"

"It is becoming an issue as you become more aware of it," says another after an uncomfortable silence. "The management style [of the pension fund] would naturally move in the direction of maximizing returns regardless of social or ethical issues. Now perhaps that's a management style we want to take a look at as teachers. But we're caught if we do. Ethically, we owe the young, our sons and daughters and students, opportunity, but we need a good return on our investment to ensure our retirement."

And that's it in a nutshell. As workers become more aware of the kind of investments being made by their pension funds, they are becoming more uncomfortable. The truth is that they would rather not know. With working people and unions getting hammered from every direction, the few success stories focus on private trusteed pension plans. Statistics Canada estimates that trusteed pension plans have more than $350 billion in assets — that's the largest pool of capital in Canada, next to the chartered banks. So it seems that the same workers who are experiencing job insecurity due to downsizing, free trade, and deregulation may be benefiting as retirees from those same economic trends. And as capital mobility and the transformation from the industrial to the service economy undermine the organized power of unions, a possible new source of power is emerging: pension fund power. The debate inside the labour movement about what to do with it is growing. With the election of Ken Georgetti as president of the Canadian Labour Congress in the spring of 1999, the use of pension fund capital may emerge as the major labour issue for the millennium. As president of the B.C. Federation of Labour, Georgetti played a major role in getting unions to use part of their pension funds for socially progressive investment.

Money is power in a capitalist society. As long as the corporate elite maintains its control over economic development, there are limits to the deepening of democracy. Public policy is influenced not only by threats to pick up and move factories to other countries, but also by more subtle threats of decreased investment. Only alternative economic development on a large scale can help to counter this corporate power, and union pension funds could provide a source of such economic development. The fact that unions have access to huge amounts of capital suggests new possibilities for economic alternatives that could be controlled at the community level.

The American management guru Peter Drucker estimates that in 1992, 50 percent of the share capital of large corporations in the U.S. was held by institutional investors, pension funds, and mutual funds. Experts estimate that in Canada, the numbers are similar. Drucker calls it the unseen revolution. "Pension fund capitalism will become the universal ownership mode in the developed countries," he says in *The Pension Fund Revolution*. If socialism is about workers owning the means of production, Drucker says, then the U.S. is already a socialist country. Karl Marx would turn over in his grave.

The issue that had the teachers' focus group tongue-tied and many of the union leaders looking at their shoes is whether that enormous pool of capital should be put to better use. Indeed, when Ken Georgetti was the flamboyant leader of the B.C. Federation of Labour, he made union control of pension funds a major priority. "We're trying to break the cycle of this fiscal roulette that money managers and financiers keep playing with capital, where its ultimate goal is to just seek a return and not seek productive things for the economy or to create jobs," Georgetti told the *Georgia Straight* newspaper.

On the other side are people like Robert Bertram, senior vice-president of investments of the Teachers Pension Plan Board. "[Pension plans] were *not* created as large pools of capital to be used for the betterment of society in response to the agendas of special-interest groups — no matter how well intentioned," he told an Ontario Teachers Federation meeting. "Rather, pension plans exist to provide benefits, specifically retirement income, to their members."

In between these two points of view are more shades of grey than I personally have ever seen in a political debate.

Union pension plans began with craft unions before the Second World War. Craft unions, which were based on a particular craft (plumbing, for example) rather than a particular workplace, took care of all their members' needs, from education to savings, so it made sense that they also would organize pension plans. Most of the union-run pension plans are still in craft unions.

Industrial unions, like the auto workers' and steelworkers' unions, had a different philosophy than craft unions. They saw their primary role as providing their members with free collective bargaining, not social services. In fact, many pension plans in industrial workplaces had their origins in company welfare schemes. When industrial unions came along in the 1930s and 1940s, the company plans were already there.

The first major debate on pension plans in North America took place in the 1950s, when scandal rocked the Teamsters' pension plan. (Teamster officials were illegally profiting from their members' pension money.) As a result, the UAW's Walter Reuther came up with a different approach to pension plans for industrial unions: the unions would negotiate pension benefits for their members, and the company would be solely responsible for figuring out how to meet its pension obligations. Despite the recent change in position by the labour movement towards more union control over pension plans, most plans in the industrial sector remain employer-controlled.

Periodically, major issues emerge concerning pension plans. In the 1980s, for example, teachers successfully fought to wrest their plan away from the control of the Ontario government. Twenty years ago, Conrad Black lost his fight to use the surplus from the Dominion Stores pension fund for his corporation. The court ruled that the surplus in trusteed pension plans belongs to the members and should be used to lower contributions or raise benefits.

And today, with the rapid growth of public-sector plans and the increased shareholder activism of some of these, new debates about the role of pension fund capital are starting to emerge. Recently, for instance, teachers' unions were up in arms when their pension plan provided 49 percent of the financing for the management buyout of the Sun newspaper chain. Earl Manners, president of the militant Ontario Secondary School Teachers Federation (OSSTF), told me in an interview, "We have a great concern that the management of the pension fund is out of control."

The OSSTF is one of several teachers' unions that constitute the Ontario Teachers Federation, which in turn provides half of the board members for the Teachers Pension Plan. Until recently, the OSSTF was a voice in the wilderness in its demands for more socially responsible investment, but after the Sun deal the rest of the Ontario Teachers Federation was won over. The federation's board of governors voted to express its dissatisfaction to the pension plan board about the investment in the Sun, demanded that two of the three pension plan seats on the Sun board be filled from the teachers' unions, and insisted that teachers' representatives promote a pro-union, anti–public sector editorial policy.

But even though these parts of the resolution caused the most media furor, provoking cries of freedom of the press from the same business columnists who seemed to have no problem whatsoever with Conrad Black's takeover of the majority of Canadian daily newspapers, there was another part of the resolution that could have much more impact in the world of pension fund politics. "Inform the Ontario Teachers Pension Plan Board," the resolution reads, "that while the Ontario Teachers Federation believes in the fiduciary responsibility of the Board and a high return on investment, the Pension Plan Board must be sensitive to teachers and their values when making investment decisions." Then the federation went further, and instructed the pension board to develop a policy for socially responsible investment.

Clearly, a revolution is brewing in the teachers' pension plan. But you wouldn't know it by visiting Claude Lameroux, the charming CEO of the plan. Lameroux is so sure of himself that he even tried to persuade me of the wisdom of trickle-down economics. He categorically rejects the idea of social investment. "The danger," he explains, "is that if I get a lower return, I am taking from one group of teachers to give to another. Besides, we're too big to use social screens. We own 4 percent of the Toronto Stock Exchange right now."

Earl Manners replies, "If we are that large and that powerful, why aren't we insisting that companies operate in the way we believe in? Insisting on good labour practices and respect for the environment? They set goals in terms of return on investment and insist that management meet those, so why not social or ethical goals as well?"

Robert Bertram, Manners's nemesis on this issue, explains that even if the fund beneficiaries voted in favour of social investment, and even if the Ontario government, which is a co-sponsor of the fund, agreed, "The pension board would not be required to follow it. Because . . . the board is an ethically bound trustee that must act in the best interests of all beneficiaries under the terms of the trust. . . . If we could measure social factors, they would only come into play if they enhanced financial performance."

At the end of 1995, according to a study done by the Canadian Labour Market and Productivity Centre, there were sixteen ethical and environmental funds operating in Canada, with assets of approximately $500 million, a pittance when placed next to the hundreds of billions in union pension plans. But true social investment can mean much more than the social and ethical screens (which eliminate companies with poor records on the environment, labour issues, health and safety, and so on) used by ethical investment funds.

The most dramatic example of social investment was the 1980s campaign to disinvest from South Africa. Unions across Canada demanded that their pension plans stop investing in companies that had dealings in the apartheid country. Objections by pension managers that these demands interfered with their fiduciary responsibility to seek the highest return in a prudent manner led unions to ask the Ontario Liberal government of David Peterson to change the legislation to permit such social investment. Attorney

General Ian Scott examined the legislation and decided that the law did permit this type of social investment or disinvestment.

Pension fund activists point to the success of the South Africa campaign to illustrate how powerful union pension funds can be. But John O'Grady, an independent economist and former pension expert with the Ontario Federation of Labour, thinks they're exaggerating. "This kind of shareholder activism is only useful on flashpoint issues like South Africa or to support the Cree in James Bay. On a strong issue, where there is a social consensus, a coordinated effort can be made, but otherwise the links of solidarity are not that strong. And by the time you go from union structures to pension fund structures, the impact is lost."

Nevertheless, American unions have been successfully using shareholder activism to pressure companies on a host of issues. During the J. P. Stevens strike in the United States, for example, the United Steelworkers of America threatened to withdraw funds from any investment banks capitalizing on J. P. Stevens unless the company began to take steps to resolve the ongoing labour dispute. The investment banks propelled J. P. Stevens to the table. In Canada, meanwhile, B.C. unions found that they were major shareholders in MacMillan Bloedel and used their muscle to stop the forestry giant from outsourcing to non-union labour.

But there are other avenues for more progressive use of pension funds. In this era of downsizing, economic targeting, such as happened with MacMillan Bloedel, is starting to look more and more appealing. Some argue that labour might even succeed in influencing macro-economic policy by the judicious and coordinated use of its pension funds.

Bill Clarke is a pioneer in the use of pension funds for economic and social goals. I met with the retired president of the Telecommunications Workers Union in the B.C. Federation of Labour office in the summer of 1997. Like most pension fund activists, Clarke began what became a lifelong obsession in the 1970s. In those days, most pension plans were run by management. But in the 1980s, when skyrocketing interest rates shot up the value of pension funds, unions started to look at getting more control of their own plans through participation on the plan boards. In B.C., for example, where the economy was booming and foreign and eastern capital was moving in to buy up profitable enterprises, Clarke and his like-minded colleagues wanted to stop provincial pension plans from financing outside investment. "Our money was invested in eastern banks, who in turn were investing in B.C. companies and taking the profits out of B.C. I didn't see why we couldn't invest the money ourselves."

Clarke convinced Ken Georgetti of his views, and ever since then the B.C. labour movement has been using some of its pension funds for progressive purposes. Several construction unions, for example, used a small proportion of their pension funds to build desperately needed affordable rental housing in Vancouver. Not only did they significantly increase the amount of rental housing available in the Lower Mainland, they also made an impressive return on their investment.

Still, some people on the left wing of the labour movement are nervous about using union pension funds as a lever of economic power. Sam Gindin, who recently retired as special assistant to the president of the CAW, has been a key figure in the development of the most progressive and impressive union in the country, if not the world. One of his concerns is that workers who have had to pay the costs of the economic crisis through wage freezes and lay-offs, through cuts in unemployment insurance and government services, may end up taking a hit in the one area where they have managed to improve during the tough times of the 1980s and 1990s: their pension plans. So he has come up with an idea that could have a profound impact on economic democratization. He calls it a job bank.

Like the social-democratic movement of which it is a part, the labour movement has accepted the framework established by capitalism and developed its demands for a bigger share of the pie within that framework. Unions, then, are wedded to a perspective of perpetual growth as the way of improving the prosperity of their membership. This is one reason why unions so often run into conflict with the environmental movement. It also means that unions are placed in the position of supporting the growth of the corporation, which provides jobs, in an era when it is getting harder and harder for workers to win a fair share of the pie. All that matters to the CEO is profit and shareholders.

In his hilarious book *Downsize This*, the American iconoclast Michael Moore tells a story about the limits of profit. If General Motors was making $7 billion in profit, Moore asks an American corporate executive on an airplane, and could make $7.1 billion by closing a factory in Parma, Ohio, would it be okay to close it? The executive answers that not only would it be fine, but it would actually be their duty to close it. It has nothing to do with morality, says the businessman; it is strictly business, and in business profit is supreme.

"So here's what I don't understand," writes Moore. "If profit is supreme, why doesn't a company like General Motors sell crack? Crack is a *very* profitable commodity. For every pound of cocaine that is transformed into crack, a dealer stands to make a profit of $45,000. The dealer profit on a two-thousand-pound car is less than $2,000. . . . GM doesn't sell crack because it's illegal. Why is it illegal? Because we, as a society, have determined that crack destroys people's lives. It ruins entire communities. It tears apart the very backbone of our country. That's why we wouldn't let a company like GM sell it, no matter what kind of profit they could make. . . . Then why do we let them close our factories? *That, too,* destroys our communities."

Moore makes the morality clear, but if it were really a matter of morality, we wouldn't find ourselves at the turn of the century with this level of poverty and inequality. In the history of capitalism, changes to benefit the majority were made only when there was a strong counterpoint to the power of capital. Today, corporations have us convinced that if we don't let them do exactly what they want, they will just pick up and go somewhere else. As long as they have all the economic power, it is difficult to find strategies to counter this blackmail. But I believe Sam Gindin has developed such a strategy.

In an unpublished paper written for the CAW, Gindin writes: "In fighting for alternatives, we need an alternative way of looking and thinking about the economy — an economics that lets us approach issues based on our own assumptions and goals. Rather than starting with the corporation as the 'unit of analysis,' we'd start with the community or the sector. Our focus, therefore, wouldn't be how to make Ford or CN stronger, but how to have an auto or rail sector, and how to develop jobs and skills in our communities. Based on this, our goal isn't to be competitive, but to *develop the capacity to address our needs*. To orient economic activity to all the people, their needs, and their future capacities — rather than leaving us subordinate to the priorities of the elite — is another way of saying we want to *democratize* economic development."

Historically, the left has looked to the state to achieve similar goals. In Canada, Crown corporations developed the railways, hydro-electricity, and other important industrial priorities. Unfortunately, these massive public corporations were run like private corporations, with an accountability often to a corporate board. No citizen feels any more ownership of Ontario Hydro than she does of Bell Canada. Theoretically, such corporations are run in the interests of the public rather than in the interests of profit, but in practice they are most often run by their own bureaucracy in its own interests.

The right argues that public corporations are inefficient because they don't have the discipline of profit. Putting aside for the moment tremendous failures in the private sector like that of real-estate giant Olympia and York, whose financial difficulties have cost tax-payers a small fortune, we can concede that profit creates a certain discipline. Unfortunately, it is a discipline that functions in the interests of a tiny economic elite. That elite can be convinced to limit its greed only by the power of a counterforce. At the turn of the last century, for example, that counterforce was the impoverished working class, who organized trade unions that fought for and won a tolerable life, including the eight-hour day and a decent share of the economic pie. In the postwar period, it was the threat of communism, as well as the demands of working men coming home from war. In the 1960s and 1970s, it was the power of the youth and women's revolutions that forced changes. Today, economic democratization is once again becoming central to the demands of young radicals.

So how can we achieve this economic democratization? Community economic development has arisen in the past few years as an alternative to massive concentrations of economic power, whether private or public. Yet although some excellent projects have emerged on the local level, they do not provide an alternative for large numbers of people or a way to pressure capital to behave differently. The National Investment Fund may.

Under the terms of the National Investment Fund, an idea developed by the Canadian Labour Congress, every financial organization, including banks, mutual funds, and pension funds, would be levied for a small percentage of its assets. This money would then be made available to fund local and regional job-development banks. This could be an exciting new way to access the massive amounts of capital that are now in private hands for priorities that we set within our own communities. The money would pay less than the market rate but provide a fair and safe return, perhaps 2 percent above inflation. Individuals like me who feel uncomfortable investing in mutual funds could buy National Investment Bonds and put as much of our retirement savings as we wanted into providing better jobs in our communities.

Gindin proposes that the fund would have a government-appointed board of directors with the responsibility for allocating the funds according to regional and sectoral priorities. I believe, however, that the administration of such a board would have to be more democratic than government appointees. The local boards that would be the recipients of these funds should be able to elect representatives for the national board, as should the financial institutions that are providing the funding. A certain number of government representatives would ensure accountability to the public at large.

The idea of a National Investment Board counters a lot of the concerns about taking union pension money away from retirees to put it in the pockets of those still seeking work. Since the return on investment would be guaranteed, there is no major risk to pension funds. Since only a proportion of pension funds would be used, fund managers could still invest the rest in higher-return investments. Finally, since all financial institutions would be required to contribute, it would mean that unions would be using their capital to leverage additional capital from private institutions rather than taking all the responsibility themselves.

The National Investment Fund also solves the dilemma of our teachers' focus group. They can provide for their future as well as contribute to the future of their children. Moreover, it gives individuals like me, who contribute an enormous amount of money to mutual funds every year, a socially progressive alternative. And perhaps most important, such a National Investment Fund would provide a significant pool of capital that could provide funding for projects based on community need rather than profit.

Gindin goes on to develop an idea of how such funds could be used in the community. He wants to see the formation, at the municipal level, of Community Development Boards. The mandate of these boards would be to guarantee everyone an opportunity to participate either in a paid job or in training/education. The principle here is similar to the one that governs school boards, which were established to ensure that everyone got an education. In the case of Community Development Boards, we would be saying that everyone in the community has the right to a job or to prepare themselves for a job. The board members would be elected and would supervise a number of institutions involved in research, disseminating information, carrying out training, holding public information meetings, and fostering public dialogue.

The board members would be elected from the community. Each board would do a needs assessment in its community, matching the economic and social needs with the workforce needs. Instead of relying solely on market forces, these boards would provide a different approach to economic development. A job or training for every citizen would be the bottom line, instead of profit.

Gindin explained his idea further in an interview with me. "They'd have to start quite modestly, because figuring out how to make decent jobs happen is something we obviously don't yet know much about," he said. "The point of this direction is to focus on this weakness and develop, over time, solutions that work. Eventually, the idea is to develop the capacity to do some planning at the community level that coordinates needs and jobs." Among the possibilities he suggests:

> Obtain from the municipality a list of all the things that must be done to maintain or improve the neglected infrastructure (e.g., housing, roads, parks, schools, hospitals).

> Invite people to submit proposals on services the community needs but is not providing (e.g., childcare, adult education, delivering medicine/food/entertainment to the aged, environmental clean-up and protection).

> Initiate steps that will prevent the loss of jobs that already exist or that will facilitate expansion of those jobs (before a plant can close, for example, investigate the reason; if technological help or temporary financing is the key, provide it).

"Let's elaborate a little on the last example," says Gindin. "We're not going to get far in creating new jobs if we can't even hang on to the jobs that we already have. At first, we might be limited to only developing some understanding of why plants close. Then we might reach the point where we can intervene in a constructive way. At some point, we might be able to go further and lead a move to convert workplaces that would otherwise close into workplaces making new products. Developing along this line would mean that we start with a few accountants who can go in and check the books of a company threatening bankruptcy, but over time we might have a research centre linked to a university that includes some marketing and technological skills, or a conversion centre that looks at new possibilities related to import substitution or new directions linked to environmental imperatives. We might also want to have an educational component, so workers/unions could learn how to figure out whether their company is not investing or keeping up and some intervention can begin before it's too late."

I would add to Gindin's model the inclusion of broader forms of decision making in the community, perhaps on the model of Brazil's participatory budget. The Community Development Board could hold public dialogues about the various options that face the community, so as to have the broadest possible discussion of priorities. Positions on the Community Development Board should be for limited terms, to ensure that a new bureaucracy is not created and that the board stays close to the community.

The combination of a National Investment Board and a local Community Development Board would make community economic development a real alternative. It is a way of democratizing capital and providing a more democratic model for publicly funded economic development. The funding is controlled at the national level to ensure standards and fairness, but priorities for investment are decided at the local level. The money used does not come from taxes but rather from the institutions that have benefited most from this newest stage of finance capital. It provides a way to divert some of the mega-profits from investors to the community. Community Development Board successes would put pressure on private corporations to do more for the community as well. In fact, the research resources of the Community Development Board could provide direction for private interests that were looking for profitable investments in the community.

Obviously, private financial institutions would resist the formation of a National Investment Bank. But the idea of community-based, democratically controlled job-development boards could provide just the vision we need to mobilize the community in support of such an alternative.

12

MORE APPEALING POLITICAL PARTIES

I N 1986, I RAN FOR PRESIDENT OF THE ONTARIO NDP (the president leads the internal mechanisms of the party) as part of a group of people calling ourselves Campaign for an Activist Party, or CAP. It became the most widely supported left-wing organization in the NDP since the Waffle. The support we had in the party membership and the way in which the party brass treated us illustrates the problems of democracy in the NDP, which is by far the most democratic of the mainstream parties.

"If we are going to change society," said a CAP brochure, "the NDP should root itself in the energetic social movements which are fighting for equality, justice, solidarity and peace. By stressing principles and activism, we can sharply distinguish our party from the Liberals in words and deeds, and in so doing, significantly broaden our electoral base."

CAP didn't really want to take over administration of the party, so we ran only a partial slate of fifteen candidates for the party executive. We did not run anyone for leader or provincial secretary, so the party leadership would understand that we were not trying to take over.

A few weeks after we announced our slate of candidates, Bob Rae's executive assistant, Robin Sears, asked to have lunch with me. As Sears's nickname among NDP staff was Vlad the Impaler, I didn't expect a pleasant lunch, but what he had in mind surprised me. He wanted to make a deal. If I was willing to change a number of things about our campaign — the two I remember were to soften my line on abortion and to cut loose the group of Trotskyists that were supporting us — Sears was prepared to offer me a spot on the official slate. That way, I could run for president on the major issues we wanted to raise but still be accepted by the mainstream of the party. Sears also tried to convince George Ehring, who was a party vice-president at the time, to resign from the CAP list with the same offer. Ehring declined and so did I.

This is a good example of how political parties work. If someone shows she can garner any reasonable support for changes in the party, the leadership attempts to co-opt that person. If that person can't be co-opted, then she is crushed. We had certainly shown that we had support. In the final weeks before the annual convention, more than 200 party members had signed a public list of CAP endorsers. This list included three Ontario Federation of Labour vice-presidents; two future cabinet ministers, Frances Lankin and Tony Silipo; the feminist Kay Macpherson; the Metro Toronto councillor Jack Layton; and many riding association presidents. Since we had this level of support and had also declined Sears's invitation to be co-opted, the party organized massively to defeat us.

When CAP nominated me, no one else had been running for party president and Gillian Sandeman, the current president, had decided to step down. When the party brass was unable to convince any one of a number of high-profile party women to run against me, Sandeman agreed to change her mind and threw her hat back in the ring. Then the party leadership tried to attack me for running against another woman.

Next, the leadership tried to stack the convention with delegates who would defeat us. In fact, there were more delegates at that Hamilton convention than there had ever been at a non-leadership convention. In those days, the CAW was supporting Rae and the mainstream of the party, and its leaders brought more than 300 delegates to the convention. Sandeman got 818 votes, I got 361. The usual attendance at Ontario NDP policy conventions was less than 800. All those extra delegates had been organized to defeat us. In my convention speech before the vote, I looked over the hall and said, "Who says the left never does anything for this party financially?" (The extra delegates all had to pay to attend the convention.) No one laughed because the tension in the room was thick enough to cut with a knife.

Our campaign had been careful never to be disloyal to the party. Even then, the spectre of the Waffle, which had been branded a party within a party, still haunted the NDP, and the people I was working with wanted to be sure that the party could not tarnish us with that kind of accusation. Nevertheless, the mainstream of the party came down on us like we were a major threat. Because of their overreaction to our campaign, they ultimately lost many valuable militants, such as Michael Shapcott, who went on to become an important leader in the anti-poverty movement in Toronto. Maintaining total control of the leadership of the party was more important to them than the contribution of the people who had supported our campaign. The NDP has always tolerated mavericks — as long as they don't organize an opposition.

A more recent example of the fear and loathing of democratic process inside the NDP was the leadership race in 1997. Going into the convention, Svend Robinson was leading in the popular vote (held in ridings before the convention) and had the support of the majority of convention delegates. Robinson had run on quite a left-wing platform, and he'd managed to attract a large number of young people to support him. At the convention, I remember thinking that I hadn't seen more young people there since I was in the Waffle in the early 1970s.

Before the first round of voting even began, it was obvious from delegates on the floor that Robinson would likely come first, Lorne Nystrom would come second, and Alexa McDonough would come third. If that was how it played, McDonough would have to drop off after the first ballot. Then Robinson would have a very good shot at winning, because half of McDonough's support came from feminists in the party who probably would have supported him over Nystrom. Nystrom supporters, on the other hand, would never have supported Robinson, because he was on the opposite side of the party. It would have been a very close vote, a vote that certain party backroom folks were not prepared to see. Even before that first vote took place, Robinson whispered to me, "They'll never let me win, Judy." And he was right.

Some of McDonough's organizers rushed over to Nystrom's camp and convinced enough of his supporters to vote for McDonough in the first round so that Nystrom would come in third, ultimately guaranteeing Robinson's defeat. Now, there is nothing illegal about such organizing, but it almost never happens. Delegates support their first-choice candidate on the first ballot and then, if necessary, move to another candidate on the second ballot. In this case, however, certain party leaders were not willing to let democracy take its course. When, in the interests of party unity, Robinson withdrew instead of going to a second ballot, he unfortunately rubbed salt in the wounds of his young supporters. I'm pretty sure most of those young supporters have now dropped out of the party. They are no doubt exercising their political volunteerism in advocacy groups now. Young people, especially on the left, are getting more and more alienated from the party process.

If political parties, and the NDP is the most democratic, behave in such a heavy-handed, top-down manner, how can they lead a government that acts differently? Reform of political parties has to be a central element of any democratic process.

Of course, I'm not saying anything new here. The Lortie Commission, which was formed in response to widespread political cynicism in the 1980s, is one of those royal commissions whose recommendations are still sitting on the shelf. The commission released its report in 1991, after extensive consultations across the country. The two-volume report and numerous background documents provide a comprehensive and quite moderate approach to political reform. Here is what the report said about political parties:

> Canadian experience, as well as that of other countries, demonstrates that a competitive political party system is an essential complement to the institutions of government. In this sense, political parties are primary political organizations.
>
> Politics is inherently adversarial because basic human passions — including self-interest and the pursuit of power — are at play. The fundamental task of governance in a free and democratic society is to restrain these passions. Citizens may organize themselves for political purposes into organizations such as interest groups or pressure groups. But only political parties can reconcile and accommodate diverse and competing interests to reach agreement on public policy.

Although I might have argued it differently, the Lortie Commission put its finger on the importance of political parties: They are the only mechanism we have to develop a program of public policy. When democracy works, the parties develop distinct programs that can compete with each other for public support. Sadly, politics in modern times has developed in a different direction. "The impact of modern communications technologies, especially television, has focused public attention on party leaders . . . and enabled if not forced parties to conduct highly professional campaigns through the mass media," says the report. "In the process, party membership has declined in importance, other than for periodically selecting candidates and leaders."

The goal of the Lortie Commission was to shore up the legitimacy of our first-past-the-post, party-based political system in face of the challenge from populists of both the left and the right. A 1989 Gallup report showed that public respect for and confidence in political parties was in steep decline. In 1979, 73 percent of people had expressed respect for and confidence in political parties, with 28 percent expressing "a great deal of respect." By 1989, those figures had declined to 65 percent and 18 percent, respectively.

Lortie suggested several ways to counter this decline. First, he argued that even though parties were private institutions, their importance to democracy required a certain amount of government regulation. In fact, he pointed out that in many countries, including the United States, government regulation of the internal affairs of political parties was more extensive than in Canada. Moreover, the state subsidized parties and candidates through tax credits and reimbursement of election expenses, providing another reason for more public regulation.

But the Lortie Commission also sought to strengthen the role of political parties. The report noted that while levels of political volunteerism and activism were relatively high in Canada, membership in political parties had been declining. This is no less true today. In the 1998 Ekos poll on citizen engagement, only 39 percent of respondents felt that it was important to participate in a political party; for voluntary organizations, the figure was 69 percent. Only 9 percent regularly participated in the activities of a political party, while 25 percent regularly participated in voluntary organizations. "The dilemma," said Lortie, "is that the core of the party organization is concerned primarily with elections; it is much less interested in discussing and analyzing political issues that are not connected directly to winning in the next election or in attempting to articulate broader values of the party." Lortie believed that the health of our democracy depended on more people getting involved in political parties. As a way of achieving this, he recommended public funding for party institutions that would focus on long-term policy development rather than short-term electoral policies.

Such institutions in other countries, said Lortie, provide the space to re-examine policy directions in a way that does not imply an immediate change in policy; they also give the party leaders a method of dialogue with both experts and citizens on policy issues and provide a buffer zone in which party leaders, legislators, and citizens can interact and communicate. Unfortunately, I believe the Lortie Commission's proposal for a policy institute would solve very little. Party life would be much more interesting if there were policy debates and discussions at the riding, provincial, and national levels, as there once were in the NDP. But if the caucus wants to do only what is politically expedient, as the NDP caucus has been doing for quite some time now, party activists tire of the energy it takes to organize for a particular policy.

Sadly, Lortie's brave attempts to broaden the scope of political parties utterly failed. One reason was that neither the Tories nor the Liberals really wanted to make any democratic changes, and even Lortie's modest proposals were too much for them. However, Lortie's approach is still very much an elitist one. Instead of looking at what people are actually doing and restructuring political life to reflect where people choose to devote their time, Lortie tried to severely restrict the role of third parties, or voluntary organizations, and make political parties do a U-turn. In the end, the only recommendation that governments picked up on was to limit third-party advertising in elections to $1,000, a move that was later overturned in the courts as unconstitutional. Today, the Chrétien government is trying once again, in current electoral-reform legislation, to implement restrictions on third-party advertising.

Lortie was correct, however, in saying that one of the reasons why interest groups have become so central to political expression and participation is because the political lives of the parties have become so degraded. Over the past twenty years, it has been the interest groups that have become the primary source of new policy thinking. Advocacy groups from the women's movement to the Canadian Taxpayers Federation, not to mention right-wing think-tanks like the Fraser Institute, have been the source of most of the new ideas that have been implemented in the political arena. In fact, it was the influence of social movements like the women's, environmental, and gay- and lesbian-rights movements that persuaded corporate Canada that it had to organize its own interest groups and policy institutes to also influence public policy. Today, political parties have become little more than electoral machines. The way to make the system more democratic is to bring citizens more directly into the political process, not necessarily into the parties themselves.

Our parliamentary system emerged out of the British system, which was based on class interests. The British Tories represented the capitalist class and the Labour Party the working class. The Labour Party even had organizational links to the trade-union movement to formalize its class connection. In a capitalist society, such organizational links were essential to keeping the Labour Party from completely caving in to the pressures of the liberal elites that so dominate the structures of the state and media. And so it is no accident that Prime Minister Tony Blair's embrace of neo-liberal politics included dramatically weakening the Labour Party's links with the labour movement. This was an organizational reflection of the liberalization of Labour's politics.

Lortie blamed modern communications, especially television, for the decline of political debate. But it is not just the communications revolution that has caused the centralization and elitism of political parties, it is also neo-liberal politics itself, which at heart represents the interests of a small elite but dresses itself in the garment of public interest. In their book *The End of Parliamentary Socialism: From New Left to New Labour,* the Canadian academics Leo Panitch and Colin Leys look at how one very important group, led by Tony Benn, a long-time British socialist, tried to transform the British Labour Party into a modern democratic-socialist party that could speak to the sensibilities of the post-1960s generation and had a strategy to combat the ferocity of neo-liberal capitalism.

Panitch and Leys argue that Benn's vision of the Labour New Left was "a much more far-reaching, active and inclusive kind of democracy than anything currently known to the British state or the British Labour Party." And, they say, it was to defeat this vision that a right-wing faction of the party crushed democracy and moved towards the accommodation with Thatcherism that today is celebrated as the New Labour of Tony Blair.

In the 1960s, the New Left influenced the Labour Party in the same way it did every other social-democratic party in the world. But the difference in the British Labour Party was that one national leader heard what the young radicals were saying and gave their ideas clearer shape and purpose. Tony Benn's experience in government, when combined with a remarkably early perception of the political forces that would eventually result in Thatcherism, enabled him to develop a coherent economic and political strategy out of the cacophony of ideas emanating from the New Left. Rather than seeing the radicalism that was reflected in industrial unrest and the black power, women's, and student protest movements as a threat to the Labour Party, he recognized the need to transform the parliamentary system to reflect the new realities. "[We need] equally radical changes in our system of government to meet the requirements of a new generation," he said in a speech in 1968. "I am not dealing with the demand for the ownership and control of growing sections of the economy. I am thinking of the demand for more political responsibility and power for the individual than the present system of parliamentary democracy provides. . . . Beyond parliamentary democracy as we know it we shall have to find a new popular democracy to replace it."

In 1973, Benn also predicted the direction the economy would take in the rest of the century. Noting that the assets of the nation's banks and financial institutions represented four to five times the total government expenditure, he asked a Labour Party convention, "Do the British people really want a society in which industrialists and bankers have more power over Britain's economic future than the government they elect?"

The End of Parliamentary Socialism outlines Benn's efforts, as minister of industry in the mid-1970s, to develop an alternative economic strategy based on industrial democracy and controls over finance capital. The book also details the New Left's initially successful efforts to democratize a hidebound bureaucratic party. But in the end, it was these efforts that provoked the strongest opposition from the party leadership.

The New Left succeeded in winning the majority of the Labour Party to its key platforms and won important democratic reforms in the late 1970s and early 1980s. Contrary to the mainstream version of Labour history, leftist policies were popular in Britain in 1980 and throughout most of 1981, despite ferocious media attacks against the "loonie left." Labour was leading in the national polls, and municipal Labour governments were implementing many of Benn's ideas at the local level. It took the Falklands War, a split to the right in the Labour Party, and the weak leadership of Michael Foot to sweep Margaret Thatcher and her Tories from their lowest level of popularity in British history to a landslide victory in 1983.

Under the leadership of Benn, the Labour New Left understood that only an alliance between parliamentary and extra-parliamentary forces could further the goals of socialism. That meant a transformation of what Panitch and Leys call parliamentary paternalism, and this proved to be more difficult to achieve than anyone could have imagined. In the end, instead of modernizing by opening the party and the state to the new democratic forces that were resisting the Thatcher agenda, Labour's leadership chose to professionalize the party through spin doctors and pollsters. The result was Tony Blair's so-called Third Way, which was not only a social-democratic embrace of neo-liberal politics, but also the transformation of Labour from a relatively democratic organization representing the working class into a top-down, elitist party.

Throughout my lifetime I have watched political parties in Canada transform themselves into professional spin machines more concerned with polls than policy and principle. The New Democratic Party was the last to fall prey to this modern corruption. In fact, the NDP used to pride itself on being as much a movement as a party. But that has changed, especially in provinces where the NDP has held power.

It was to counter this shift towards the elitism that transformed the Labour Party that we first formed CAP. In fact, the Campaign for an Activist Party had at its heart many ideas similar to Tony Benn's. CAP believed, for instance, that instead of behaving like the other parties, the NDP should make a closer alliance with the movements fighting for equality, a cleaner environment, the eradication of poverty, and so on. But the party tended to see a deep divide between these movements and itself: the job of these movements was to organize extra-parliamentary pressure on the government, and the party's job was to get state power. CAP's idea was to foster a more equal relationship, where the party and the movements would decide priorities together and influence each other. We also saw the need for the NDP to become more active in extra-parliamentary campaigns. By using party resources for campaigns led by social movements, we believed, party activists would be more closely integrated with social activists and the party would be more accountable to the needs of the people. We knew even then that the NDP was becoming professionalized like the other parties. And without a structure that would permit grass-roots activists to counter the pressure imposed by the professional pollsters and spin doctors, the party was doomed to drift to the right.

What has become clear to me since those CAP days is that the only hope for a social-democratic party that wants to continue to fight for socialism is to restructure and democratize. A left-wing party cannot claim to speak in the interests of working people if it is not organized to get the broadest possible input from those working people. Indeed, one of the most lasting effects of the radicalization of the 1960s is that citizens want more control over the democratic process. That the right has manipulated this desire into right-wing populism does not reduce its importance to any progressive transformation of society.

Unfortunately, the social-democratic left took the ideas of social equality and environmentalism from the New Left, but resisted the idea of participatory democracy. This resistance to democracy inside the parties is then reflected in their resistance to the democratization of the state. Most social-democratic leaders, like all other professional politicians, believe they know what is best for the people. They also fear that if more direct democracy is introduced into the system, left-wing ideas will suffer. Ironically, this fear of popular rejection of the left is a major reason for its marginalization, certainly in Canada and the U.S. There are parties in Europe that have done it differently, however, most notably the German Greens and the Danish Socialist People's Party.

In March 1979, various organizations and movements in West Germany united to form the Further Political Association (FPA), which later became the Greens. The new organization's name made it clear that these movements had no intention of giving up control to the "party." Initially, the FPA wanted to run only a limited electoral campaign for a nuclear-free Europe and a decentralized Europe of the regions. The idea was to create a "parliamentary voice for the social movements," movements that in the past had won massive public support only to have their demands ignored in the German parliament. But slowly the party grew, and in 1983 it had an electoral breakthrough and a significant number of members were elected to parliament. After many years of successes and failures, the Green Party is today in coalition with the German social-democratic party, SPD, although it has unfortunately lost many of its most democratic features.

The Danish Socialist People's Party (SF) started as a majority breakaway from the Communist Party. Its initial platform was based in part on democratic issues that arose after the Soviet repression of the Hungarian uprising in 1956. In the 1960s and 1970s, the party had cornered 11 percent of the vote and was operating with an open and democratic process. Social activists joined and transformed the party in a way that CAP would later seek to transform the Ontario NDP. The new activists also won the leadership of the party, and they proceeded to form coalitions with social movements on an equal basis. Hilary Wainright's assessment in her book *Arguments for a New Left* is that "in Denmark's municipalities, where the ecology and women's movements are a lively part of daily life, these movements are also, through co-operation with the SF, guiding the decisions of the municipality." Nevertheless, says Wainright, the SF is still overwhelmingly dominated by its parliamentary section.

The German Greens and Danish Socialist People's Party show that parliamentary parties can have a positive and symbiotic relationship with social movements. In Canada, where most social movements guard a non-partisan political stance, this can be more difficult. But if most grass-roots activism is in advocacy groups, it is essential that a left-wing party have a closer and more equal relationship with them.

In the 1980s, I was actively involved in the Ontario NDP because I believed that social movements alone could not bring about social change. Today, political power is still located in the state and political discourse focuses primarily on what governments are doing. Of course, advocacy groups can have an impact on the agenda, as the women's movement did for many years. However, without access to a political party that shares at least some of their values and issues, advocacy groups are limited in what they can accomplish.

In her book *Women on the Defensive: Feminism in Conservative Times*, Sylvia Bashevkin points out that of thirty decisions on women's groups' claims made during the tenure of Brian Mulroney, more than 85 percent were pro-movement; this includes nearly 90 percent of Supreme Court judgements and more than 80 percent of legislative action. In the U.S. under Ronald Reagan, less than half of the thirty government actions on women's issues were consistent with feminist demands. While Bashevkin credits the Charter of Rights and Freedoms for much of the success in Canada, I believe that the support of the NDP had an important impact because the party took many of the demands of women's groups into the House of Commons. Bashevkin's book does not document women's demands during the Chrétien government's term of office, but my own experience would indicate that women have won much less, in part because parliamentary opposition was primarily coming from the right, which is traditionally hostile to feminism.

In *The End of Parliamentary Socialism*, Panitch and Leys argue that the Labour left was the last gasp of parliamentary socialism. But ironically, they claim that it was the nature of parliamentary democracy itself that thwarted the success of the New Left. Given the hostility of the media to the economic and political ideas of the Bennites, Panitch and Leys point out, it would have taken time to win the support of the British public. Unfortunately, the emphasis on short-term electoral victories precluded such a strategy. This is the other side of the argument that the right wing of the NDP makes. They, together with the media, always pose the debate between those in the party who are practical and want to win elections, and therefore support more moderate policies, and those who want to stick to NDP principles and support more left-wing policy. The media, in turn, always paint this as a struggle between those who want to modernize the party and those who are stuck in the past.

Yet I believe that the NDP's shift to the right has actually cost it electoral support. In fact, with the exception of Roy Romanow's NDP in Saskatchewan, where there is no significant Liberal Party, the party has never succeeded by appearing to be more like the other parties. Bob Rae's upset victory in Ontario in 1990, for example, was won on a clear social-democratic platform.

The story is the same for the federal NDP. Its eradication in 1993 had at its heart two factors. First, the willingness to jump into bed with the Conservatives and Liberals on the Charlottetown Accord made it look like just another mainstream party. As a result, countless western NDP votes went to the Reform Party.

Second, the betrayal of Bob Rae's government in Ontario also cost the federal party. Thomas Walkom, in his book *Rae Days*, places a lot of the blame for the 1993 federal electoral debacle on the Rae government for its right-wing policies. "In Ontario, all nine New Democratic MPs lost their seats and the party's share of the popular vote crashed to an almost unbelievable 6 percent," he wrote. The Ontario NDP's pollster at the time, David Gotthilf of Viewpoints Research in Winnipeg, told the *Kingston Whig-Standard*: "I've tried to persuade my NDP clients across the country that they're better off positioning themselves as viscerally populist, very much talking in the language of class. Language like 'Make the Rich Pay' might scare some of the membership of the board of the *Globe and Mail*, but it plays very well with NDP constituencies."

B.C.'s Glen Clark won his election in 1996 on a clear social-democratic platform in which he said he was strongly on the side of working people. After the election, however, he quickly moved to the right. When his support plummeted to 18 percent in the polls, party and labour activists insisted that the only way he could recover support would be to move back to the left where he belonged. Moving right gets the NDP more media attention, but it has never got the party more electoral support.

Nevertheless, almost all social-democratic parties are under intense pressure to conform to the mainstream approach, to become centralized and professionalized and more moderate. Ironically, even the right-wing Reform Party was forced to make these kinds of changes in its quest for political power. In fact, when I attended a Reform Party convention in London, Ontario, in the summer of 1998, I was struck by its similarities to NDP conventions of the 1980s.

The Reform assembly was a cross between a Christian revival meeting and an oddly clipped NDP convention. The enthusiasm was palpable, not only in the convention hall but also in the corridors. The Reformers were very nice. They welcomed me. They shook my hand. "Just want to tell the folks back home that I shook hands with Judy Rebick," one said to me. They furtively told me that they like the CBC. They remembered my role in opposing the Charlottetown Accord and congratulated me on it. One young woman said she had even joined NAC because of Charlottetown, "but don't tell anyone here." I asked a lot of people what they like about Reform. Everyone enthusiastically explained that grass roots really led the party. There was even a "Grass Roots R Us" T-shirt for sale. I found myself thinking that in light of today's cynicism and devotion to cool, there was something refreshing about the guile-less enthusiasm of Reform delegates.

Could it be, I wondered, that the right was now more grass roots than the left? In the sixties, I belonged to a counter-culture group called Grass Roots. In those days, those of us who believed in women's equality, gay rights, and environmentalism felt alienated from the mainstream culture. In the 1990s, it's those who believe in the traditional family, women's place in the home, and conservative Christian values who feel alienated. In the Reform Party, these people have found a home. This, I think, is the essence of the resist-ance to Manning's attempts to open up the party. If he lets those hip, urbane federal Tories into the Party, will the grass roots still feel like they belong?

In truth, as the Reform strategist Ric Anderson tries to turn the party into the slick political machine it needs to be to win power, the "Grass Roots R Us" people will have to be suppressed, just as Tony Blair suppressed the Labour left. If Reform and the Tories merge, the social conservatives who now form such an important base of the Reform Party will be silenced, just as the left inside the NDP was silenced. I don't think either scenario is good for democracy. The more political parties become like each other in their efforts to win power, the more people on the right and left sides of the political spectrum will feel excluded.

The Reform Party managed to recuperate a lot of the rage that Keith Spicer reported was in the land in the early 1990s. They chan-nelled rage against lack of accountability in government into rage against government, the public sector, and those who depend on the public sector. I heard Ric Anderson say on CBC's "The House" that there are a lot of people in the Reform Party who want to be the right-wing NDP, and these people will resist every attempt to broaden the base of Reform. I think what is more accurate, how-ever, is that these people will resist every attempt to make Reform less democratic, less grass roots, and more accountable to the media and the corporate elite than to its own membership.

Some commentators would say that eliminating the extremes of political parties and moving everyone closer to the centre is a positive thing. I disagree. The clash of ideas is fundamental to democracy. What passes for debate these days is whether the balanced budget should be achieved in one year or five years, whether tax cuts should be 20 percent or 30 percent, whether $2 million or $3 million more should be contributed to health care.

The powerful pressure on political parties to move closer to the centre can be countered by structuring the parties to ensure more grass-roots democracy. The difficulty is that the burden of the quest for power limits the degree of democracy. Political parties are hesitant to air their dirty laundry before an increasingly nasty media. Party activists are persuaded that conventions should be more of a photo-op than a full, open, and sometimes passionate debate. I think the only solution for a left-wing party is to rely on closer ties with community and advocacy groups and on an increase in extra-parliamentary activity. Just as we have discussed in other chapters, structured influence from people at a grass-roots level is the best way to counter the pressure of the corporate, media, and bureaucratic elites that are always trying to mould political parties in their own image.

13

A Democratic Electoral System

ONE OF THE MOST UNUSUAL COALITIONS in Canadian history came about during the run-up to the Charlottetown Accord, when the National Action Committee on the Status of Women, of which I was president at the time, and the Western Triple-E Senate people, many of whom supported the Reform Party, joined together to support proportional representation (PR) as a way of electing the new Senate. Even the Mulroney government supported the idea, but the provincial premiers, who were actually negotiating the accord, nixed it as soon as they took the discussion behind closed doors. It has recently re-emerged as a new policy initiative for both the Reform Party and the New Democratic Party.

I came to the idea of proportional representation during the 1988 election, when I first realized how truly undemocratic our electoral system was. Everyone agreed that that election was virtually a referendum on free trade. Yet ironically, the majority voted against free trade but somehow still elected a government that favoured it. Fifty-two percent voted for the NDP and the Liberals, parties that at the time were ferocious opponents of free trade, and only 43 percent voted Conservative. Yet Brian Mulroney rode to victory with almost 60 percent of the seats.

Lest anyone think I am a sore loser, I'll say right now that I think the election of the B.C. NDP government of Glen Clark was even worse. There the NDP won a majority of seats with only 39 percent of the vote; the Liberals had significantly more votes than the NDP but got only 45 percent of the seats.

And even our current federal Parliament bears little resemblance to the wishes of voters across the country. In the last election, the Liberals got only 38 percent of the popular vote but ended up with 52 percent of the seats in Parliament and 100 percent of the power. Although the Liberals claim to be the only truly national party, it was the concentration of the Liberal vote in Ontario that won them their majority. And even then, they won all but two seats in that province with 49 percent of the popular vote. The two right-wing parties together had 38 percent of the popular vote but got only one seat between them.

When you look at the popular vote across the country for the Reform Party and the Tories, the results are even more lopsided. Both parties won 19 percent of the popular vote, but Reform became the official opposition with sixty seats and the Tories stayed in last place with twenty. Reform actually got more votes in Ontario than it did in Alberta, and yet it won all but two of the Alberta seats and none in Ontario. And we call this democracy.

Our current electoral system — generally called first past the post or winner takes all — is an anachronism that was created with the birth of liberal democracy centuries ago and has since been discarded by almost every democracy in the world except Britain, Canada, and the United States. This electoral system favours big parties and regional parties. In Canada, we have had countless majority federal governments since 1945, but only two of them actually won a majority of the votes.

All other Western democracies have turned to proportional representation, where the number of seats more closely reflects how people actually voted. In a pure PR system, a party that gets 38 percent of the vote would get 38 percent of the seats. If we had proportional representation in our current federal Parliament, the Liberals would have had to make an agreement with one of the opposition parties to stay in power. Such a situation may or may not have produced a better government, but it would certainly have produced a more accountable one.

The biggest argument against proportional representation is that it creates unstable governments. But with the Liberals seemingly permanently ensconced in Ottawa, a little instability in government seems like a pretty good idea to me. Anyway, Germany, Sweden, Iceland, and Switzerland don't seem that unstable, and they all have PR systems. And of course, any instability in the PR system can be minimized by raising the minimum vote threshold to 3 or 4 percent. In other words, a party must get at least 3 percent of the vote before it can elect a single member. That way, smaller political parties with significant voter support can be represented in Parliament. If representatives of the Green Party, the Christian Heritage Party, and (as in Iceland) a Women's Party were elected to Parliament, imagine how much more interesting and representative Parliament would be. Instead of wasting years trying to unite their two very distinct parties, Reformers and Conservatives could form a coalition government if they got enough votes. Instead of encouraging the bitter divisions on the left about how and when to support the NDP, those disillusioned with the rightward turn of social democracy could form a democratic socialist party that could be more than a quixotic dream. Instead of losing their identity inside a larger party where the majority dominates the public agenda, differing currents could put their particular positions forward without sacrificing a chance at power. Think how much more interesting and democratic politics would be.

In the Netherlands, the minimum vote threshold is .67 percent. In Germany, it is 5 percent. The Netherlands has a staggering twenty-four parties in its legislature, but only four parties would get elected if the threshold was increased to 3.5 percent. Of course, it is possible to form a new party under our current electoral system.

We have brave fringe parties that put forward candidates every election, but they don't have a hope in hell of ever electing any of them. This encourages somewhat wacky candidates like those from the Rhinoceros or Flying Yoga parties but discourages serious political people who know that without a regional base, such as has been carved out by the Reform Party and the Bloc Québécois, it is almost impossible to reach the level required nationally to elect members. The first-past-the-post system favours regional parties: they can become well enough known in that single region to get elected.

Of course, not all systems of proportional representation are the same. There are different versions, and these must be evaluated before implementation. In a PR system, you vote for a list of candidates instead of an individual candidate. The differences in different systems are in how that list is developed. In the party list system, the party develops a roster of candidates and ranks them in order of importance, with the party leader at the top. When you vote for all or part of that list, you must accept the order that the party has set. This is similar to our current system, where parties choose the candidates for whom we vote. In each PR constituency — let us say that the Lower Mainland, Vancouver Island, and south-central and northern B.C. are the constituencies — each party would make up a list of candidates. Voters would select, say, ten members of Parliament from their region. They could choose from each party list, accepting the party ranking. Some would vote for the entire party list, but others would not. Let's say, for example, that I wanted the NDP to be the government, but I thought the party was weak on environmental issues. I might then vote for seven NDP and three Green candidates. I would, however, have to vote for the top seven NDP candidates. The ten candidates who receive the most votes in that region are elected.

Some criticize this system because it takes power away from local party ridings and places it in the hands of the party leadership. But this concern could be dealt with by electing the party list at a general membership convention and ranking those on the list according to votes received. This system works best for demographic representation. Parties under pressure, whether it's the pressure of law or of public opinion, are much more likely to make sure that their lists are fully representative of women, racial and ethnic minorities, and geographic regions.

Another system, which is promoted by Nick Loenen in his book *Citizenship and Democracy*, is the single transferable vote (STV). This is a more complicated but much more democratic system where the voters themselves rank the candidates regardless of which party they represent. Under this scenario, a well-known figure like Maude Barlow could run for a tiny party and still get elected because of her personal popularity. Since the voters and not the party's leadership or membership have the power to rank individuals, the party apparatus would be severely weakened. The focus would be more on the individual candidate and less on the leader. In fact, even party discipline would be severely undermined, because MPs would not owe their position to the party brass.

While in some ways this scenario may sound like a dream come true, in other ways it would be enormously open to corruption, as is the case with the American system. I believe that there is too much party discipline today, but undermining it can lead to gridlock and too much influence for lobbyists, who can buy individuals more easily than they can parties. The SVP system would also exacerbate the cult of celebrity. With individuals more important than parties, we would probably end up with even more focus on personality than policy. Finally, it is a very complicated system. If people in the last Ontario election had trouble understanding strategic voting, I am afraid SVP would have their eyes glazing over.

In Germany, they have a mixed system, which we might prefer in Canada, at least while we're making the transition to PR. We could double the size of our single-member constituencies, then elect half of our MPs the old way and the other half through PR. In Germany, they use different systems for their two houses of government, which is also something we could try. The problem here, though, is that it might create two classes of MPs, with those elected by PR representing a larger number of constituents and having more freedom from their party leadership. Our NAC/Triple-E proposal for PR for the Senate would have given us a similar system to Germany's.

Whichever system of PR is chosen, it will be infinitely more democratic than the system we have in Canada today. And not coincidentally, all the countries in the world with the best representation of women in government use PR as their electoral system. In fact, the pioneer feminist Doris Anderson has been a strong supporter of proportional representation for years. "It's fairer, it doesn't knock out little parties, and it represents minorities better," says Anderson. "There is a wider range of parties, so the government is often a coalition, which makes government more co-operative," she adds. "A prominent Liberal once told me, 'All we have to do is get elected every four years and then we can do whatever we want.'" Anderson thinks that kind of attitude would disappear in a PR electoral system.

Indeed, demographic representation would improve no matter what PR system we chose. And that can only be a good thing, for while almost everyone agrees that the Canadian electorate is profoundly dissatisfied with politicians, they fail to acknowledge that a significant part of this alienation is a result of the fact that most politicians are so removed from the daily realities of their constituents' lives. The spectre of a male-dominated Parliament voting on an abortion bill, an almost all-white Parliament dealing with issues of racism, or a Parliament where most members are financially secure tackling poverty and unemployment is surely as abhorrent as that of a Parliament dominated by central Canada voting for resource taxation in Alberta. A Parliament that better mirrored the life experience of the electorate by representing voters in terms of gender, class, race, and region would no doubt be closer to the concerns of the people. Regional interest and party affiliation are the only identities deliberately represented by our current system. Most people I know, even outside of Ontario, identify themselves in many other ways that could be better reflected through a PR system.

The observation that our current electoral system is the height of representative democracy could be made only by groups of white professional men, who dominate the editorial boards as well as the Parliament. The barriers to women and other under-represented groups in the nomination process has been well documented in the report of the Lortie Royal Commission on Election Reform. With no spending limits, no public assistance in financing, and a variety of selection criteria that favour white, middle-class men, nomination battles raise almost insurmountable barriers for most women, minorities, poor people, and others. To counter this, Lortie recommended spending limits and public reimbursement for nomination campaigns. Although this would certainly help to level the playing field in contested nomination battles, a PR system would have a more dramatic effect on the number of women and minority MPs.

Yet despite all these potential benefits, support for proportional representation in Canada has until recently been pretty fragile, with the strongest support coming from smaller parties, such as the Green Party, whose only chance of actually winning a seat would come through electoral reform. Those in power who benefit from the undemocratic first-past-the-post system want to keep it, whatever their political stripes.

But PR seems to be getting new life. The veteran Saskatchewan NDP MP Lorne Nystrom tabled a private member's bill last year proposing an all-party committee to examine the different methods of proportional representation and then present a proposal to the people through a referendum. "We're sleepwalking towards a crisis in democracy," said Nystrom in an interview. "When I was first elected in 1968, voter turnout was 78 percent. In the last election, it was down to 67 percent. People are more and more alienated from the democratic system." What appeals to Nystrom is not just the possibility of better representation of the people's will at election time, but also the possibility of a better reflection of people's lives between elections. The NDP convention in the summer of 1999 adopted Nystrom's proposal.

Nystrom is not alone. The Reform Party adopted a formal position in favour of a Canada-wide referendum on proportional representation at its convention in the spring of 1998. Ted White, a B.C. Reform MP and the party's direct democracy critic, says this position will now go into the Blue Book as official party policy. There are not too many other issues where the NDP and Reform are in agreement. The problem, of course, is that the Tories and Liberals have benefited so mightily from the current system that nothing short of a mass movement would convince them to change it.

Nevertheless, in B.C., Reformers and NDPers are participating in a cross-party coalition called ECCO, which is engaging in popular education and organizing support for a PR system. In central Canada, Democracy Watch also supports a PR system, but it has been unable to get backing across the political spectrum. Still, the deep chasms that exist between the left and the right on economic and social issues are no reason why there cannot be an alliance on democratic issues like PR. The bitterness of right-left struggles in the past ten years would make such a coalition difficult, certainly, but not impossible.

Internationally, everyone is doing it. Australia and New Zealand both now have versions of PR. The recent elections in Northern Ireland were conducted with a PR system, and Prime Minister Tony Blair has recommended it to Scotland and Wales for their next elections. Roy Jenkins, a senior British cabinet minister, is even heading up a parliamentary commission to examine changing Britain's system to PR. Word has it that the change will be brought in after the next election. Then only Canada and the U.S. would be stuck with the old British system. Isn't it time we joined the twentieth century and adopted a democratic electoral system too?

Nevertheless, for proportional representation to be genuinely democratic, we have to reduce, if not eliminate entirely, the influence of the real special interests, those with a hand of control on government: the corporate class. That is why the restructuring of party financing is one of the most important political reforms.

Democracy Watch issued, in June 1999, a report with seventeen recommendations for cleaning up party financing. Instead of maintaining the current system of tax-deductible political donations, which the Liberals have just increased, Democracy Watch, along with many other advocates of electoral reform, suggests a system of public financing based on the actual popular support that parties win. This would ensure that parties never receive financing based on their ties to wealthy corporations. "The democratic principle of one person, one vote should be extended to the political finance system to ensure that those with money do not distort Canada's political process," the report says.

Direct public financing of political parties would also make the tax money they receive more transparent. Most people don't realize, for example, that political parties received $30 million in public money in the last election (they are reimbursed by the government for 22 percent of what they spend on a campaign). The increase in the reimbursement rate that has been proposed in the new electoral financing legislation would make that $40 million. But there is no reason why the money that is given now as tax deductions and reimbursements for campaigns couldn't be transformed into direct funding. Political parties could still raise money but without tax deductions. A lot of people now don't even take the tax deduction, and no doubt would continue to contribute without it. I think it is a good proposal, as long as there is a minimum available to any party, so that new parties could have access to this funding prior to running in an election.

A more immediate demand, which Democracy Watch also supports, is a ban on corporate and union financing of political parties. They argue that entities that cannot vote should not be permitted to finance parties. In our system, corporations are indirectly buying political favours from the parties in power.

The corruption of corporate funding is nowhere clearer than in Mike Harris's Ontario, where electoral financing reform is going in the opposite direction. Political parties can now spend $4.2 million on an election campaign; the limit was $2.7 million before the Tories were elected. In 1995–97, the Ontario Conservative Party raised $27.7 million, which compares with $10.8 million for the Liberals and $8.8 million for the New Democrats. According to a study by the York University political scientist Robert MacDermid, most of this money comes from rich people and corporations. "How well a society controls and diminishes the structural advantage of the wealthy is a measure of its commitment to democratic principles and political equality," MacDermid writes. Although Harris is fond of accusing the unions of using their money to influence politics, they actually contributed only $445,282 to the NDP from 1995 to 1997. If we compare this with the $11,853,958 contributed by corporations to the Tories in the same period, we can only wonder what special-interest group is really running Ontario.

Before the 1999 election, Harris changed the financing rules to suit his own purposes. Contribution limits were raised to $7,500 per year to the central party and $5,000 to constituency organizations. According to MacDermid's study, the increase in maximum donations means almost nothing to the individual contributor. In 1996, for example, just twenty-two individuals gave $4,000 to the PC central party. So why increase the maximum? The answer is obvious. Big corporations, 228 of which gave the maximum in 1996, will be able to buy themselves even more influence with the Harris Tories. MacDermid says, "The evidence suggests that the changes will benefit only a small percentage of corporate donors and a minuscule percentage of individuals, most of whom have ties to those same corporations." He also points out that while the changes benefit the Tories, they will strongly encourage other parties to focus their fund-raising efforts on the same large donors. Since the NDP recently dropped its own restrictions on accepting donations from corporate donors, even it may try to woo the big money. Finally, the increase in maximums will accelerate the cost of election campaigns. Harris also increased the spending limits here.

Tax laws also favour corporations. Individuals can reduce their taxes by only $750 for a $4,000 donation. (This will increase if new federal election-spending laws come into effect.) However, a corporation can deduct the entire $4,000 from its Ontario taxes. The corporate tax credit also allows a company to carry forward any unused portion of the tax credit to future years if its Ontario taxes are less than the value of its contribution. Since Ontario corporate taxes are only 10 percent of federal taxes, this means that corporations can avoid provincial taxes altogether by making large enough political contributions. For those who want to argue that it is none of our business how much corporations give to political parties, MacDermid estimates that $9 million in tax credits flows to donors to the Ontario Tories. That's a lot of tax money.

Corporations already have a massive advantage over everyone else in the political arena. They have the money to hire spin doctors and lobbyists. They have the time to spend with bureaucrats and politicians to convince them of their point of view. They have the class connections with the media magnates, which in turn make a press bias much more likely. They have the power to threaten to move their plants or offices elsewhere if governments don't meet their priorities. On top of all that power, why should they be given so much additional power in party financing? A ban on corporate funding of political parties is essential to any truly democratic government. Quebec has done it, and that province manages to run election campaigns just fine.

We could require television stations to provide more free advertising time to political parties to reduce the cost of election campaigns. And perhaps if they didn't have quite so much money to run paid ads, political parties might spend more time meeting directly with voters or subjecting their leaders to interviews by skilled journalists. This, too, would have a salutary impact on electoral democracy.

There are other important issues around election financing too. Duff Conacher of Democracy Watch points out that the financing system in Canada is much less transparent than that in the United States. The biggest loopholes are with the riding associations and the leadership campaigns. In fact, Jean-Pierre Kingsley, the former head of Elections Canada, once called riding associations the black hole of election financing because they are not required to disclose the names of their donors. Individual members of Parliament are also not required to disclose donations received in non-election years. Disclosure is required for political parties, but it is done in a way that makes tracking donations very difficult.

In the U.S., party financing is tracked quarterly and published on the Internet in a fully searchable format. In Canada, it is done only once a year and interested parties have to go down to Elections Canada and pore over print books. Only someone as dedicated as Conacher would bother. In the U.S., all parties must provide the names, addresses, and employers of donors. In Canada, only the name is required, which means that an employer could get around spending limits by getting his employees to donate. And without addresses, it is difficult to know if one individual is giving more than the legal limit.

Democracy Watch also has a good proposal for how to govern the spending of third parties. This is the only part of the Lortie Commission report that the federal government has tried to implement. Its first attempt to restrict the spending of advocacy groups and other interest groups during elections to $1,000 was struck down by the Supreme Court. In the new federal electoral financing bill, the government has restricted spending to $150,000, which is more reasonable but still problematic if third parties want to advertise during elections. Of course, if there are spending limits on political parties, there should certainly be spending limits on third-party advertising during election campaigns. Otherwise the level playing field that is created by election-spending rules is completely obliterated by third-party spending, especially when it targets a particular party or candidate. On the other hand, limiting third-party spending too much eliminates these groups from the electoral arena altogether. Many Canadians participate in elections through their work in advocacy groups, so excessive restrictions on the participation of these groups is anti-democratic. Democracy Watch suggests that third-party spending be limited to a certain amount per member. That way, interest groups with few members but lots of money, such as the Business Council on National Issues, would not be able to outspend groups with a lot of members but not so much money, like the Council of Canadians.

Another major issue raised by Democracy Watch is ethics in political lobbying. Duff Conacher says the current code of conduct for lobbyists is toothless. Howard Wilson, the government ethics counsellor, contacted 192 parties in preparing the consultation on the code, reported Democracy Watch. "Only 28 of the parties could be categorized as representatives of citizen groups or individual citizens. In contrast, 87 associations representing business interests, 50 major corporations and 27 government-relations consultants were contacted." Needless to say, the proposal to develop a stronger code of behaviour was rejected by those consulted. Here's an excellent example of how participatory democracy would make a huge difference.

The code does require a lobbyist to inform Wilson if he is doing work for the government and also representing a client who is lobbying the government. But as long as the two parties involved feel that the conflict is not a problem, then it is fine. The worst offender on this score is the Earnscliffe Group in Ottawa. This company advises Finance Minister Paul Martin on presenting his budget and also has clients who lobby Martin on that budget. This should be forbidden, according to Conacher. "If you are lobbying, you shouldn't have any relationship with the government." In Ontario, people like Leslie Noble and Tom Long, who orchestrated the successful Tory election campaign, are making oodles of money as consultants to people who want to influence the government. This should also be illegal.

Conacher proposes the need for an ethical watchdog. Instead of reporting to the prime minister, as Wilson currently does, the watchdog should have the same independence from the government as the auditor general does. In fact, in 1994 the auditor general himself proposed that he be given the role of ethics counsellor. Whether or not he is ultimately given the job, it seems obvious that we need much stronger conflict-of-interest guidelines for lobbyists, as well as an independent ethics watchdog.

There is no shortage of proposals on how to make our electoral system more representative, transparent, ethical, and accountable. All that is missing is political will. From the Lortie Commission to Democracy Watch, advocates of electoral reform are trying to make the system more representative of the voting public. But only a massive movement for democracy will persuade those in power to loosen their reins to allow a truly democratic system to emerge.

EPILOGUE

PERHAPS YOU HAVE READ UP TO HERE and are thinking, Oh, sure, these are great ideas, but they will never happen. Power is just too entrenched to ever let these kinds of changes come to pass. People are too self-interested; they don't really want more direct participation in the democratic process. Most people are just interested in themselves and their families.

One of the most stunning moments of my brief career as a visiting professor at the University of Regina in 1994 was the day that a young man in my class asked, "What's the point of fighting for social change? You've been fighting for twenty years, and things are worse now than they were then." In some ways they are, but in some ways they are not. The status of women, for example, which was my focus for much of that time, has been completely transformed.

I'm fond of telling the story about when I graduated from McGill University and applied for a job writing news for a private radio station. This was the entry-level job of that time and my mostly male colleagues on the *McGill Daily* were all applying.

"We don't hire girls," the station manager explained to me.

"Why?" I asked.

"Because the men swear in the newsroom, and they wouldn't be comfortable with a woman there."

"I don't give a shit if they swear," I replied, and now I was doubly damned: not only a woman but a foul-mouthed one at that.

That was in Montreal in the spring of 1967. Not that long ago. But things changed because of women like me rebelling against such treatment, getting together and organizing against the big and little indignities and injustices we suffered daily. No man was going to give up even a tiny share of power if all we did was ask politely. And governments were no more friendly to a women's rights agenda in the 1960s than they are today to the deep democracy ideas developed in this book. In the late 1960s, when Prime Minister Lester Pearson was asked if he would appoint Pauline Jewett to the cabinet, he answered, "Oh, no, we have one woman already." The resistance of the powerful to women's rights can be measured by how slowly women rise in their ranks, especially when compared with the speed of their gains at other levels. Yet through fighting for our rights in all the ways that we did, and through turning that struggle into a fight for equality, feminists around the world have forced the power elites to change, indeed even to begin the process of their own transformation — at least in gender terms. Organizing can and has changed the world.

To be sure, some things have changed for the worse since I was in university, but for women everything has changed for the better. And generations before mine fought for and won workers' rights and other once-unimaginable protections and entitlements. The people in power do not easily make changes that threaten that power, but they'll never make any changes at all unless there is a massive and well-organized movement to counter them.

That movement, I believe, is already forming around the world. I have argued that this anti-corporate movement — along with the movements continuing to fight for economic and social equality, peace, and ecological sanity — needs to focus on bringing more people into active participation in the political arena. And all these movements must bring in not just people who are in agreement, but also all the people who have so little opportunity to share their political wisdom in ways that are meaningful. Still, I've learned enough from my years of activism not to argue that active citizenship is the only important issue facing progressive people. I have had too many arguments with those who told me that if the world blows up, feminism will mean nothing, or that if we poison the planet, wages and working conditions will make no difference. Resistance to the cancerous plague of greed that is sweeping the elites around the world is essential. Continuing to expand the horizons just newly created for women, gays and lesbians, and people with disabilities is inevitable and inspiring. Deepening the struggle against racism until everyone understands that it pervades our society and nothing short of a transformation will rid us of its mean, thieving ways is central to any struggle for democracy. Never have I felt the importance of the environmental movement more than I do now, with the dangers of bio-genetics, agra farming and corporate fishing, weird climate changes, and epidemic respiratory illness among children. All of these movements need to embrace participatory democracy, not only in their own ranks but in society as a whole.

People already in the corridors of power have an interest in this too, including backbench MPs, public-service workers at every level who know better how to do things but never get a chance to say so, journalists who would rather be doing something more meaningful and connected, and honest politicians.

But mostly this transformation will benefit those who have never participated in political life beyond voting and keeping up with current affairs. The day the Supreme Court of Canada struck down the abortion law was the most joyous moment of my life to that point. And so I understand that there are few feelings more satisfying than knowing that you, along with others, had a direct impact on changing the world for the better. Working with others in a common cause is another excellent feeling. That genius that Tom Paine noticed is inside of us all — it's time for political liberation.

We need a political movement that unites everyone in fighting for an expansion of democracy. Unlike Preston Manning, I don't think you can combine an expansion of democracy with fiscal conservatism. The rule of the market is of necessity anti-democratic. There it is those with the most money who have the most power. Expanding democracy means that those with the most power will have to share more of it and probably even have to give a fair bit of it up.

That the right has tapped into the interests of Canadians in more direct forms of democracy is a credit to them. But their democratic vision is limited by their economic principles, which ensure a pyramid-shaped society rather than one built more in hills and dales. A democratic platform that includes economic democratization is needed more than ever before. And we need not wait for an existing political party to take up the cause, any more than we needed to wait for an existing political party to take up the cause of women's liberation.

Paternalistic democracy has outlived its time. The people are ready to take more responsibility in governing themselves. If our governments are on the road to accepting self-government for aboriginal people, why not keep going?

The rule of the father is starting to be democratized in our families, in our communities, and in our culture. Why not continue the democratization into our political system? It's not enough just to have more people play the role of the father. We learned that in the women's movement. If nothing else changes, then it changes nothing to have women in some of the powerful roles. We have to transform the patriarchal rules of governance.

The rule of the rich and powerful has not been as strong as it is today since the early days of capitalism. If it is not countered by the interests of the majority, the future for most of us will hold much less than the present. Youth movements around the world are already beginning the struggle to restrict unbridled corporate power and to create alternative visions of a more egalitarian, eco-friendly, peaceful, and just society. Women are uniting across the globe to fight against the scourge of poverty and violence. Resistance to the new robber barons, who seek not only money but the very elements of life, is widespread, especially in the East. Yet most of you probably don't even know about these movements. We need to open up the democratic space so we can learn from those who do not have power in the world.

In closing, let me summarize the model of active citizenship as:

- combining of direct and representative democracy;
- establishing an electoral system of proportional representation;
- valuing the wisdom of everyday life;
- including citizens at every level of decision making;
- allowing referenda on central issues;
- decentralizing and democratizing the administration of the state;
- having experts on tap rather than experts on top;
- inviting people to participate directly in the decisions that affect their lives;
- reducing the power and influence of the corporate elite;
- electing politicians to work co-operatively with the citizens they serve;
- making the process of decision making central to the right decision;
- redesigning democracy to be bottom up more than top down;
- including all demographic groups, especially those most marginalized in our current system;
- valuing voluntary organizations as a primary vehicle for citizen participation;
- ensuring more accountability for political parties and paid lobbyists;
- establishing citizen watchdog groups composed of the users of major public and private services; and
- creating an adequately funded public broadcaster and more accountable private media.

To enable participatory democracy, we need to:

- urgently address and reverse the growing gap between rich and poor;
- open up and democratize international institutions;
- reduce the work week; and
- create pools of capital that can be democratically invested in the community based on community priorities.

At the beginning of the twenty-first century, it is time to complete the democratic revolution. As John Lennon once sang, "It's easy if you try."

INDEX